PublicServicePrep Comprehensive Guide to Canadian Forces, Border Services and Corrections Exams

COMPREHNSIVE GUIDE TO CANADIAN MILITARY, BORDER SERVICES AND CORRECTIONS EXAMS, published by:

PublicServicePrep
http://www.publicserviceprep.com
info@publicserviceprep.com

Authors:
Deland Jessop, Kalpesh Rathod, and Adam Cooper.

ISBN 978-0-9735151-9-0

Printed and bound in Canada

Table of Contents

Introduction

Welcome to PublicServicePrep. The application process for government jobs can be very competitive. We understand the situation you're in and the challenges that lie ahead for you. This study guide was developed to help you prepare for the public service exams used by government bodies across Canada.

By purchasing this guide, you have taken the most important step - you have moved from thinking about preparation to taking action. Your dedication to preparing for your entrance exams demonstrates that you are the motivated person government services want to hire.

If you are looking for more practice tests and further preparation materials, visit our website at WWW.PUBLICSERVICEPREP.COM. We offer a special discount of 25% for those who have purchased this guide. When signing up online input the following code in the referral code section to get the discount (note the code is case sensitive):

ppdc0712

Please do not hesitate to contact us if you have any questions, concerns or comments about this book, our website, or the application and testing process. We will be happy to do anything we can to assist you.

Phone: 1-866-765-4237
Email: info@publicserviceprep.com
URL: http://www.publicserviceprep.com

Preparation Material

Resume Building

A resume is a tool you can use to demonstrate your fit for the job-specific requirements of a career. Few people have received instruction on building a resume, or had much experience writing them. They don't understand what should or should not be included to present themselves in the best manner they can.

Resume building does not start at the writing stage. If you are serious about applying for a government position, you should have a long list of volunteer experience, academic achievements, languages, computer skills and other highlights to place on your resume. If you don't, begin today. Many organizations, including food banks, charity organizations and Children's Aid Societies are desperate for volunteer help. Languages, especially French are important for government agencies, as are computer skills and any other life skills.

The main purpose of your resume is to frame your experiences, skills and knowledge in a manner relevant to the position to which you are applying. You have to not only demonstrate what you've done, but also show that you have done it well. It is crucial to present information clearly and concisely so the person reviewing your resume can quickly find what they require. Three principles should be followed:

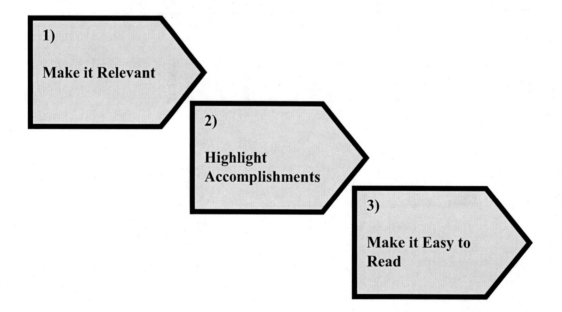

1) Make it Relevant

2) Highlight Accomplishments

3) Make it Easy to Read

Principle One: Make it Relevant

Government agencies want to fill positions with people who fit their needs. It is important to determine what competencies are required for the job. Below is a sample list of competencies that may be useful for many government jobs.

Analytical Thinking	The ability to analyze situations and events in a logical way, and to organize the parts of a problem systematically.
Self – Confidence	A belief in your capabilities and recognition of personal limitations.
Communication	You must have the skills to effectively communicate using listening skills and verbal and written communications skills.
Flexibility / Valuing Diversity	With government jobs, you will have to work with a wide cross-section of the community with diverse backgrounds, cultures and socio-economic circumstances. You must have the ability to adapt your approach to each situation.
Self - Control	You must establish that you can control your emotions and actions when provoked.
Relationship Building	Developing contacts and relationships both within and outside your area of employment is extremely valuable.
Achievement Orientation	You must demonstrate a desire for continuous improvement in service and accomplishments.
Information Seeking	The ability to seek out and consider information from various sources before making decisions.
Assertiveness	The capacity to use authority confidently and to set and enforce rules appropriately.
Initiative	Demonstrated proficiency to be self-motivated and self-directed in identifying and addressing important issues.
Cooperation	Willing to act with others by seeking their input, encouraging their participation and sharing information.

Negotiation / Facilitation	The ability to influence and persuade others by anticipating and addressing their interests and perspectives.
Work Organization	The ability to develop and maintain systems for organizing information and activities.
Community Service Orientation	Proven commitment to helping or serving others.
Commitment to Learning	Demonstrated pattern of activities that contribute to personal and professional growth.
Organization Awareness	A capacity for understanding the dynamics of organizations, including the formal and informal cultures and decision-making processes.
Developing Others	Commitment to helping others improve their skills.

Many people squeeze everything into a resume hoping that something will click. Any material on your resume that does not exhibit traits from the list of core competencies the agency is looking for is a waste of space.

Do not include every employer on your resume unless you are specifically asked to provide that information. Many government agencies require an employment history application. Pick out the most relevant positions you have had and focus on demonstrating the qualities. Any additional information such as Activities, Volunteer Experience, Education, or Special Skills should also demonstrate your competencies.

Principle Two: Highlight Accomplishments

Accomplishment statements should give your potential employer an indication of how well you performed. It should reveal not only what you did, but also how well you did it. Each statement should include the following:

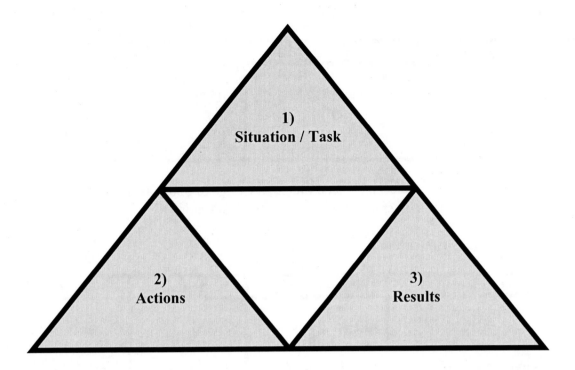

Each accomplishment should describe skills relevant to the job you're applying for. Practice writing these statements. Typically, accomplishment statements fall under the Work Experience, Volunteer Experience, or Education sections of your resume.

Example Action Statements

1) Day Camp Counsellor

Core Competency	Situation / Task	Action	Result
Developing Others, Cooperation, Assertiveness, Community Service, Communication.	Field trips as a day camp counsellor.	Instruction and supervision.	Ensured safety of 60 children with fellow counsellors.

"Supervised and instructed 60 young children on field trips ensuring their safety and enjoyment with a team of fellow counsellors."

2) Retail / Grocery

Core Competency	Situation / Task	Action	Result
Work Organization, Communication, Negotiation / Facilitation	Controlling Inventory.	Organized units and placed orders (quantified)	Diverse customer's needs anticipated and satisfied.

"Organized shelving units and placed orders in excess of $20,000 ensuring diverse customer needs were anticipated and satisfied."

3) Post-Secondary Education

Core Competency	Situation / Task	Action	Result
Initiative, Achievement Orientation, Analytical Thinking, Commitment to Learning, Communication	Attending post-secondary education.	Studied sociology (or any other major)	Graduated with a strong standing, developing a core set of skills.

"Developed analytical, presentation, computer and XXXX skills, studying sociology and graduating with a 75% average."

4) Volunteer Work

Core Competency	Situation / Task	Action	Result
Initiative, Communication, Cooperation, Work Organization, Developing Others, Self-Confidence, Flexibility / Valuing Diversity, Negotiation / Facilitation, Community Service Orientation	Food drive at work.	Organized and implemented.	Raised $2,000 for needy people in the community.

"Organized and implemented a Food Drive with a team of volunteers, effectively raising $2,000 for needy people in the community."

Action Verbs to be used for your Accomplishment Statements

Accelerated	Displayed	Negotiated	Saved
Accumulated	Documented	Ordered	Scheduled
Accomplished	Effected	Organized	Selected
Acquired	Enforced	Performed	Separated
Analyzed	Engineered	Perpetuated	Served
Applied	Evaluated	Planned	Set
Arranged	Facilitated	Prepared	Shared
Assessed	Filed	Prescribed	Showed
Authorized	Financed	Presented	Solved
Approved	Founded	Problem-solved	Strengthened
Began	Generated	Processed	Succeeded
Bought	Hired	Produced	Supplied
Budgeted	Identified	Promoted	Taught
Coached	Implemented	Provided	Team-built
Collected	Invented	Questioned	Trained
Combined	Launched	Raised	Translated
Communicated	Learned	Read	Tutored
Conducted	Made	Realized	Uncovered
Convinced	Maintained	Reorganized	Unified
Coordinated	Managed	Repaired	Utilized
Developed	Marketed	Researched	Vitalized
Directed	Minimized	Revised	Won
Discovered	Monitored	Risked	Wrote

Principle 3 - Make it Easy to Read

Recruiters may look at thousands of resumes each year. They do not necessarily spend a lot of time on each one. This means your resume has only a few minutes to prove that you are a good fit for the job. The information presented has to be immediately pertinent and easy to read. Key things you should be mindful of when finishing up your resume are:

- use high quality bond paper
- incorporate as much white space as possible so the reader is not overwhelmed
- highlight only key words or positions to attract attention
- use bullet points rather than paragraphs
- keep font sizes between 10 and 12 pt

Language and grammar are very important to a resume and the following should be observed:

- make every word count
- use short, simple and concrete words that are easily understood
- use strong nouns and vital verbs to add action, power and interest
- avoid personal pronouns
- spell check the document and always have someone proof read the material
- double check the meaning of easily confused words, i.e.:

>   affect (influence) vs. effect (result)
>   personal (private) vs. personnel (staff)
>   elicit (draw forth) vs. illicit (unlawful)
>   discreet (showing good judgement) vs. discrete (distinct or separate)
>   allude (indirect reference) vs. elude (to evade)

A few rules-of-thumb

- months do not need to be included in dates when the length of employment is greater than six months
- part-time and full-time descriptors are generally not included
- do not include names of supervisors
- check with the government service to which you are applying to about disclosing full employment history

Review the copy of the sample resume below.

Resume Components

Name	Address Telephone Number E-mail

Education

Educational Institution Location Degree	Date
Educational Institution Location Degree	Date

Work Experience

Company, Geographic Location Position title - Descriptive Statement if needed - Relevant Accomplishment Statement - Relevant Accomplishment Statement	Date
Company, Geographic Location Position title - Descriptive Statement if needed - Relevant Accomplishment Statement - Relevant Accomplishment Statement	Date
Company, Geographic Location Position title - Descriptive Statement if needed - Relevant Accomplishment Statement - Relevant Accomplishment Statement	Date

Examples of Optional Section Headings

- Professional Development - Computer Skills - Languages - Activities and Interests - Volunteer Experience	- Awards - Summary of Qualifications - Functional Skills - Publications - Academic Achievements

Jane / John Doe (EXAMPLE)
2 / 2 Wellington Crescent, Winnipeg, Manitoba   Phone: (204) 555-1212
johndoe@xxx.ca

Education

CITY COLLEGE, Winnipeg, Manitoba   (1996 -2000)
Police Investigations Diploma
- Elected Class President and managed a budget of $5,000 and a team of 15 volunteers to deliver class social activities and educational assistance programs.

MAIN STREET COLLEGIATE, Brandon, Manitoba   (1991-1996)
OSSD, OAC Certificate, Honour Roll, Senior English Award

Professional Experience

You Name It Security, Vancouver, British Columbia   (2000-present)
Security Guard
- Investigated and handled property disturbances arising from a variety of situations, and resulting in reports, cautions or arrests.
- Organized and implemented a neighbourhood watch program for clients taking a proactive role to reduce instances of break and enters in a residential complex.

Toronto Parks Department, Toronto, Ontario   (1995-1999)
Assistant Activity Implementer
- Scheduled and implemented a variety of after school activities for 50 – 60 children with fellow co-workers.
- Used a needs-based approach to assist children from diverse cultural backgrounds with a variety of problems such as schoolwork, bullying and loneliness.

Volunteer
- Thanksgiving Food Drive - annually delivering food to needy people throughout the community
- Children's Aid Society – Special Buddy Program   (1995-1998)
- City College Orientation Leader   (1999)

Interests
- Shodan Black Belt in Jiu Jitsu, running, weight training, snowboarding, rock climbing, white water rafting, sport parachuting, water skiing and SCUBA diving.
- Piano – Royal Conservatory Grade 5. Guitar - Introductory lessons.

Computer Skills
- Excel, WordPerfect, PowerPoint
- Internet development, Outlook

The Interview

It is important to recognize that government agencies are looking for the best people for the job and will not try to consciously confuse you.

At this stage it is your interpersonal and communication skills that will help you land a job. The interviewer is looking for someone who is competent, likeable and who fits in with the organization's culture, goals, beliefs and values.

What Interviewers Tend to Look For

Friendly Personality

With many government jobs, you spend a great deal of time with co-workers. Every interviewer will ask themselves whether or not they would enjoy working with you. You must prove that you are likeable enough to do this.

Organizational Fit

Many organizations may have a very particular culture and it is important for interviewers to ensure that job applicants will fit that culture. Suitability may include the willingness to work shift work and overtime if required, give up days off if required, or an ability to function well as a member of a team.

It is important not to pretend to be something you're not. If you feel you wouldn't fit in with an organization's culture, then it is probably best for both you and the organization that you seek another career. It is important to ask these questions of yourself. Once in the interview stage, you should be confident that you would fit in with the culture.

Capable and Professional

Government organizations want competent personnel. You must demonstrate that you are capable of handling responsibility and that you can perform the required tasks. It would be prudent to review any core competencies required for the job to which you are applying.

Handling Pre-Interview Stress

Feeling nervous before an interview is perfectly normal. Politicians, entertainers and media personalities feel nervous prior to performances as well. The best way to handle the stress is to be well prepared. Once again, interviewers are not trying to trick you. They want you to succeed; it makes their job easier. Some things you should do before the interview include:

- Get a good night's sleep (this goes without saying, but bears repeating).
- Practice interviewing with friends, using the behavioural questions below.
- Wear professional clothing (suits or business dress).

You should bring all of the documents that are requested from you (transcripts, copy of your resume, portfolio) to the interview along with a pad of paper, a pen, a list of references and a list of questions you may have. Interviewers are often impressed if you have intelligent and researched questions about the job.

How to Influence the Hiring Decision

Understand the Organization – Local Focus Interviews

It is important to have at least a rudimentary understanding of the organization to which you are applying. This information is available on most websites, or at employment offices where you are applying. Some information you should know would include:

- Rough size of the organization or group with which you will work. (example: Canadian Forces have 62,000 regular members, 25,000 reserve members and 4,000 Canadian Rangers)
- Name of the managers or politicians in charge of departments. (example: Ralph Goodale – Minister of Finance 2005.)
- The challenge that all government services are facing (asked to do more with less, budget constraints, intense scrutiny, etc.)

Before any interview, make a habit of reading the newspaper and checking the internet for news about the department you are applying to, so that you are aware of the local issues and concerns of the area.

Understand the Job

You have to understand the job to which you are applying. Gather as much information about the job as you can, including typical tasks, where your office would be, career paths, etc. To prove that you understand the job, make sure that you include the less glamorous duties that it might entail (filing reports, answering phones, dealing with the public, etc.).

Understand Yourself

When you are involved with an interview, it is extremely important to be very familiar with your resume and past situations in your life. You will more than likely encounter questions about your past acts, goals and emotions. The list below includes a number of questions you should be familiar with prior to any interview.

- How have you prepared for this position and what are your qualifications?
- What are your greatest strengths and weaknesses?
- How do you get along with co-workers?
- Why are you pursuing a career with this department?
- What motivates you to perform well?
- What are your three greatest accomplishments in life?
- How would you work under pressure?

First Impressions

First impressions are extremely important. Many judgements are made about a person within the first 30 seconds of an encounter (fairly or unfairly). It is your job to impress the interviewer(s). Three basic steps you can take to ensure that you make a great first impression are:

Look Professional	Be Confident	Break the Ice
Interviewers want to see an applicant who respects them enough to wear the appropriate attire.	Greet the interviewer (s) with a smile, a firm handshake, a relaxed manner and a friendly "Hello".	Engage in small talk. It can be about anything, (weather, traffic, etc). It doesn't have to be profound. It's meant to put both parties at ease.

Communication and Interpersonal Effectiveness

The interview process is a situation that tests your communication skills. You should be aware of the following:

Eye Contact	Maintain eye contact with the person you are addressing. This means looking at the person who is speaking to you. In interviews with more than one interviewer spend an equal amount of time on each person.
Body Language	Be aware of your position in your seat and your breathing pattern. Attempt to relax by taking steady breaths. Make sure you sit up straight in an interview. This will exhibit self-confidence and professionalism.
Gestures and Speech	Be aware of any gestures you use. Nod and maintain eye contact to indicate that you understand interview questions. Smile when appropriate, and be vocally expressive by alternating your tone where necessary. Be natural and avoid filler words such as "umm" and "like".

During the Interview

Make an effort to read the interviewers. Ask yourself whether they appear to be straining to follow you, if you are talking too fast (breathe more deeply), or too softly (speak louder). If they are writing frantically, that is usually a good sign, but make occasional pauses so that they can keep up. If you do not understand a question, ask them to repeat or clarify it. If you do not know the answer to one of their questions, admit it. Do not lie during the interview.

Prepare Stories Prior to the Interview

Interviewers may have some questions regarding your resume, or your past experiences. Make sure you are familiar with the content in your resume, and any tasks that you mention in it.

Many government agencies will use a behavioural-based interview method. This means that they will ask you questions about yourself and will ask you to describe events that have actually occurred in your past (usually the last two years). Some examples of questions you should be prepared to answer include:

Give an example in your life when you:

- were involved in a stressful situation and how you dealt with it.
- were extremely angry and how you dealt with it.
- had to take the role of a leader, and how was the situation resolved.
- had to work as part of a team and explain what happened.
- had to resolve a conflict with other parties and how did you handled it.
- were up against an important deadline and how you handled the work.
- had a conflict with a supervisor and how you handled it.

There are many other behavioural questions, but these are some of the most common examples.

How to Answer Behavioural Based Questions

Each behavioural question is a story about your past. Make sure that the story you tell is relevant, clear, and even interesting (interviewers are only human). Each story should have:

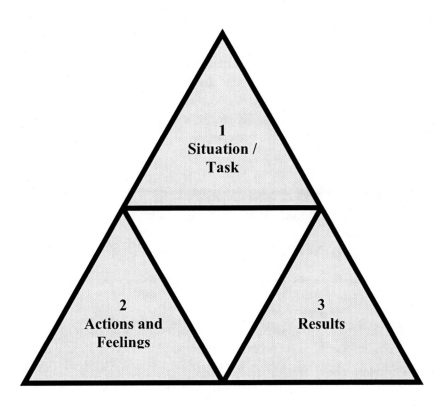

Step One - Understand the Question

This is vital. If you do not understand the question or what the interviewer is asking for, ask them to repeat it or explain it. There is no point giving a very effective answer to the wrong question. For example: one interviewee, asked about Ethnicity, spoke a great deal about Ethics during an interview. The interviewers probably thought he was an idiot, but he was probably just nervous and didn't hear the question properly.

Step Two - Brief Synopsis

Let the interviewers know what you plan to talk about with a brief outline of the situation, with little detail. This will give you some time to organize your thoughts and the interviewers will understand where you are going. This should take no longer than a couple of sentences.

> **Example:**
>
> "I am going to tell you about a conflict I had with my boss while I was working as a personal trainer. It involved a situation where I was told to bill a client at a rate I didn't feel was justified. We dealt with it away from the customer and resolved it in a manner that satisfied myself, the manager, and the client."

Step Three - Full Story

A retelling of the story will demonstrate to the interviewers your competencies in dealing with the situation and your communication capabilities. Interviewers want a clear story, preferably in a chronological sequence. They are most concerned with your feelings during the situation, the actions you took, and the result of your actions. Always finish the story with the results of your actions. Keep these points in mind both while you are preparing for the interview, and when you are participating in it:

- Answer the question asked.
- Pause and think – don't rush in with an answer.
- Pay attention to the pronouns you are using. Interviewers want to know what "YOU" did. Use the pronoun "I" for your actions and "Us" for team actions. **DO NOT ALWAYS USE "WE".** You will fail the interview.

> **Bad Example**:
>
> "We formed a team to solve the problem. We brainstormed an idea to solve the problem. We then decided on a course of action and began to implement it. We handled task "A" while others handled task "B". We all had individual assignments."

> **Good Example:**
>
> "I formed a team to solve a problem. We brainstormed an idea to solve the problem. I then had to decide the course of action and we began to implement. My friend John and I were responsible for task "A" while another group handled task "B". My particular assignment was to do "X".

- Ensure you effectively explain the situation, your feelings, your actions and the result.
- If necessary take pauses to collect your thoughts. There is no need to be constantly talking.
- Relax and enjoy telling the story. You should know it well, as you actually did it.
- Give focused and fluid answers.
- Avoid run-on answers.
- Give support for claims that are made, if possible.
- Show evidence of preparation work.

Other Interviewing Methods

You should be aware that you could be asked technical or "what if" questions or questions about your past. Some agencies may ask:

- What would you do if you caught a co-worker stealing?
- Have you ever smoked marijuana?
- Have you ever stolen anything?
- Have you ever committed an illegal act?

It is important to give these questions careful consideration and answer honestly. If you tried smoking marijuana when you were in high school, admit it and tell the interviewer why you didn't continue to use it. For example, you found it hurt the academic performance of your friends, or something along those lines.

"What if" questions are intended to challenge you, to see if you are the type of person who will immediately back down. This is not a trait agencies are looking for. Once you have made up your mind on an issue, stand by it. Interviewers may challenge you but this is part of the process. Just ensure that you give careful thought to the question to avoid defending a weak position. It is acceptable to credit the other opinion, but do not change your decision.

On top of these questions, you may receive some technical questions when applying to specific positions

Completing the Interview

Just like the first impression, it is important to give a positive impression during the last few moments of an interview. If you have any questions for the interviewers, the end of the interview is when they should be asked. It is acceptable to have prepared questions written down. As you are leaving the room, smile at the interviewer(s) individually, walk up to each one, look into their eyes, shake their hands and personally thank them for their time.

General Suggestions

Preparation Prior to Testing

Check out the websites and contact the government agency to ensure that you are familiar with the testing procedures and the content of the exams. It is important to get as much information as possible from the department to which you are applying.

Practice on numerous tests to ensure that you are familiar with the content of the testing material.

Before Testing

Get enough sleep before the tests and enough food and water even if you are nervous prior to entering the test. Try to remain relaxed and comfortable. Wear clothing that is professional, but also comfortable to work in. Arrive early and ready to begin.

During the Test

Don't waste time on a question you are unable to answer; take a guess and move onto the next question. Make a note of answers you are not certain of, and review them if you have time after answering the remaining questions.

Pay attention to the answer sheet and the question number. Many applicants have failed as the result of an error on the scoring card. Every time you respond to a question, look at the answer card carefully and make sure that the number you are answering on the card matches the number of the question.

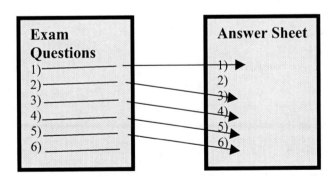

In the above example, even if the applicant answered the questions correctly, the applicant would only get one out of the six questions right because of the errors on the scoring card. Keep this in mind when taking the test. You will not be able to correct or explain yourself if you make a mistake on the score card because they are computer scored. This mistake is more common if you if you decide to skip a particular question. In the event that you decide to skip questions, a tactic to avoid making an order error is to cross off the question you skipped on the answer card.

Teaching Material Math

Addition

$$7 + 5 = 12$$ (shown in vertical form)

$$7 + 5 = 12$$

The above two equations have the same value and are very straightforward. It is important to know that the order of numbers does not make a difference in addition (or multiplication). For example:

$$6 + 3 = 9 \qquad \text{same} \qquad 3 + 6 = 9$$

$$243 + 716 = 959$$
$$\text{same}$$
$$716 + 243 = 959$$

Some complications arise when larger numbers are used and you need to carry numbers.

Note: When you see a math problem laid out horizontally, as in the box immediately above, rearrange the numbers so that they are vertical (on top of each other) to make the addition easier to do.

Example:

	(A)	(B)	(C)
3 5 1	3 5 **1**	**1** 3 5 1	**2** 3 5 1
6 9 9	6 9 **9**	6 9 9	6 9 9
+4 5 7	+ 4 5 **7**	+ 4 5 7	+ 4 5 7
	17	20 7	**15 0 7**

(A)
Start by adding up the numbers in the right most column. The result is 17. The seven remains but the one is carried over to be added to the next column of numbers.

(B)
The same rules apply to the sum 20 in the second column. The 0 remains in the second row, while the 2 is carried over to the column to the left to be added.

(C)
The final column is then added and the answer is recorded.

Subtraction

$$\begin{array}{r} 8 \\ -\quad 3 \\ \hline 5 \end{array}$$

$8 - 3 = 5$

The above two equations have the same value and are very straightforward. It is important to know that the order of numbers is significant in subtraction (and division). Different ordering will result in different answers. For example:

$$\begin{array}{r} 18 \\ -\quad 3 \\ \hline 15 \end{array}$$
different
$$\begin{array}{r} 3 \\ -18 \\ \hline -15 \end{array}$$

$$712 - 245 = \quad 467$$
different
$$245 - 712 = -467$$

Some complications arise when larger numbers are used and you need to carry numbers.

Example:

$$\begin{array}{r} 7\ 4\ 3 \\ -5\ 8\ 9 \\ \hline \end{array}$$

(A)

$$\begin{array}{r} 3 \\ 7\ \cancel{4}\ {}^{1}3 \\ -5\ 8\ 9 \\ \hline 4 \end{array}$$

(B)

$$\begin{array}{r} 6\ {}^{1}3 \\ \cancel{7}\ \cancel{4}\ 3 \\ -5\ 8\ 9 \\ \hline 1\ 5\ 4 \end{array}$$

(A)
The first task is to subtract the right most column. Because 9 is larger than 3, a unit has to be borrowed from the column to the left. The 4 in the middle column is reduced to 3, and the one is added to the right column, making the first row 13 - 9 = 4.

(B)
The second task is to subtract the second column. The same process is repeated. Borrow a 1 from the left column to allow the subtraction. The top number in the left column becomes 6, while the top number in the centre column becomes 13. 13 - 8 = 5. The left column would then be subtracted. 6 - 5 = 1.

Note: If subtracting more than 2 numbers, you cannot stack the numbers as you would in addition. Instead, work from the first subtraction to the last, two numbers at a time.

Multiplication

$$\begin{array}{r} 8 \\ \times\quad 6 \\ \hline 48 \end{array}$$

$8 \times 6 = 48$

The above two equations have the same value and are very straightforward. It is important to know that the order of numbers makes no difference in multiplication (or addition). For example:

$$\begin{array}{r} 7 \\ \times\quad 8 \\ \hline 56 \end{array}$$

same

$$\begin{array}{r} 8 \\ \times\quad 7 \\ \hline 56 \end{array}$$

$245 \times 233 = 57,085$
same
$233 \times 245 = 57,085$

Multiplication, simply put, is adding groups of numbers. For instance, in the above example, the number 8 is being added six times.

$8 \times 6 = 48$	$7 \times 7 = 49$
$8 + 8 + 8 + 8 + 8 + 8 = 48$	$7 + 7 + 7 + 7 + 7 + 7 + 7 = 49$
$9 \times 5 = 45$	$6 \times 3 = 18$
$9 + 9 + 9 + 9 + 9 = 45$	$6 + 6 + 6 = 18$

It will be difficult to pass an exam if you have to calculate all simple multiplication in this manner. You should memorize the basic multiplication tables for 1 through 12. Review the multiplication table in this book.

Some complications arise when larger numbers are used and you need to carry numbers.

Example:

	(A)	(B)	(C)

```
              (A)            (B)            (C)

                4              4  4           4  4
  2 6 7         2  6  7       2  6  7        2  6  7
  x 1 5 6     x 1  5  6     x 1  5  6      x 1  5  6
                     4 2        4 0 2       1  6 0 2
```

(A)

Begin by multiplying out the right row. The 2 is recorded in the right column and the 4 is transferred to the middle column and recorded as above.

(B)

The second step is to multiply the 6 in the middle column. 6 x 6 = 36. The 4 that was carried over from step A has to be added to the 36. The result is 40 and the 0 is recorded in the middle column. The four is then carried forward to left column as in step A.

(C)

The 6 then has to be multiplied to the left digit on the top number. 6 x 2 = 12. The four that was carried over from step B is added to the 12. The result is 16 and recorded as shown.

```
           (D)              (E)                (F)

               3               3  3            3  3
     2  6  7       2  6  7          2  6  7
   x   1  5  6   x   1  5  6      x   1  5  6
     1  6  0  2    1  6  0  2       1  6  0  2
         3 5  0      3 3 5  0     1  3  3  5  0
```

(D-F)

The next steps are to multiply the second digit in the bottom row (the 5) to each of the top digits. The 5 is multiplied to the 7, the 6 and the 2. The process is the same as steps A - C. If the number is 10 or larger the number is carried over, as above, and added to the next multiplication.

It is important to remember that the next multiplication set has to be recorded on the line below and lined up starting in the next column. Place a zero in the right column to ensure the digits line up properly

	(G)			
		2	6	7
x		1	5	6
	1	6	0	2
1	3	3	5	0
	7	**0**	**0**	

	(H)			
		2	6	7
x		1	5	6
	1	6	0	2
1	3	3	5	0
	6	**7**	**0**	**0**

	(I)			
		2	6	7
x		1	5	6
	1	6	0	2
1	3	3	5	0
	2	**6**	**7**	**0**	**0**

The next steps are to multiply the left digit in the bottom number by each of the digits in the top number. The same process is used as outlined above if numbers have to be carried over.

Lining up of the digits is also necessary at this stage. Because you are multiplying from the hundreds column (the left most) you begin recording the answer in the hundreds column. Follow the same procedure as outlined above. Fill in the first two columns with zeros.

		2	6	7
x		1	5	6
	1	6	0	2
1	3	3	5	0
+ 2	6	7	0	0
4	1	6	5	2

The final step is to add up the three numbers that were multiplied out. Treat the addition of these three numbers exactly as you would a regular addition problem. If you failed to line the numbers up properly, you will wind up with an incorrect answer. 41,652 is the final answer.

Note: Because complex multiplication questions (like the one above) involve addition, make sure you have a firm grasp of the addition section before trying to tackle multiplication.

Things to Watch For

Watch out for a multiplication question where the first digit in the bottom number is a zero, or where there are zeros in the equation. You still have to properly line up the digits. Note the highlighted zeros.

```
      3 4 5
x _____ 5 0
  1 7 2 5 0
```

Remember that zero multiplied by any other number is zero. In this situation you begin multiplying with the 10's column (the 5). Because you are multiplying from the 10's column, you begin recording your answer there. Place a zero in the first column.

```
        3
      6 0 9
x _____ 4
    2 4 3 6
```

When the four is multiplied to the 0, the result is 0. The number, which is carried over from multiplying 9 x 4 has to be added to 0, which results in the highlighted answer - 3.

```
        4 5 2
x       3 0 9
        4 0 6 8
+   1 3 5 6 0 0
    1 3 9 6 6 8
```

In this situation there is no need to multiply the bottom ten's digit out, as the result will equal 0. You must, however, properly line up the numbers. Because the 3 is in the hundred's column, you must begin recording your answer in the hundred's column. That is why there are two highlighted zeros.

Multiplication Tables

	1	2	3	4	5	6	7	8	9	10	11	12
1	1	2	3	4	5	6	7	8	9	10	11	12
2	2	4	6	8	10	12	14	16	18	20	22	24
3	3	6	9	12	15	18	21	24	27	30	33	36
4	4	8	12	16	20	24	28	32	36	40	44	48
5	5	10	15	20	25	30	35	40	45	50	55	60
6	6	12	18	24	30	36	42	48	54	60	66	72
7	7	14	21	28	35	42	49	56	63	70	77	84
8	8	16	24	32	40	48	56	64	72	80	88	96
9	9	18	27	36	45	54	63	72	81	90	99	108
10	10	20	30	40	50	60	70	80	90	100	110	120
11	11	22	33	44	55	66	77	88	99	110	121	132
12	12	24	36	48	60	72	84	96	108	120	132	144

Use of the Table

To use this table, take a number along the top axis and multiply it by a number along the side axis. Where they intersect is the answer to the equation. An example of this is 7 x 3. If you find 7 on the side axis and follow the row until you reach the 3 column on the top axis, you will find the answer – 21.

Look for simple patterns to assist your memorization efforts. For example:

Whenever 10 is multiplied to another number, just add a zero.

    10 x 3 = 30   10 x 7 = 70
    10 x 10 = 100   10 x 12 = 120

Whenever 11 is multiplied by a number less than 9, just double the digit 11 is multiplied by.

    11 x 3 = 33   11 x 5 = 55
    11 x 7 = 77   11 x 9 = 99

One multiplied by any other number is always equal to that number.

    1 x 1 = 1   1 x 4 = 4
    1 x 8 = 8   1 x 12 = 12

Zero multiplied to any number is always zero.

    0 x 10 = 0   0 x 3 = 0

Nine multiplied by any number less than 11 adds up to 9.

    9 x 3 = 27   (2 + 7 = 9)
    9 x 9 = 81   (8 + 1 = 9)

Division

$$6 \ / \ 3 \ = 2 \qquad\qquad 6 \div 3 \ = 2$$

$$\frac{6}{3} = 2 \qquad\qquad 3\overline{)6}^{\;2}$$

The above equations have the same values and are very straightforward. It is important to know that the order of the numbers is significant in division (and subtraction). Different ordering of numbers will result in different answers. For example:

$$10 \ / \ 5 = 2 \qquad \text{different} \qquad 5 \ / \ 10 = 0.5$$

$$15 \div 5 = 3 \qquad \text{different} \qquad 5 \div 15 = 0.33$$

$$\frac{100}{10} = 10 \qquad \text{different} \qquad \frac{10}{100} = 0.1$$

$$10\overline{)50}^{\;5} \qquad\quad \text{different} \qquad 50\overline{)10}^{\;0.2}$$

Simply put, division determines how many times a number will fit into another. Picture an auditorium with 100 chairs available. Several schools want to send 20 students to see a play in the auditorium. Now you need to determine how many schools can attend the play. This will require division.

By dividing 100 by 20 ($100 \div 20$) you come up with the number 5. Five schools can send 20 students to attend the play.

<u>Long Division</u>

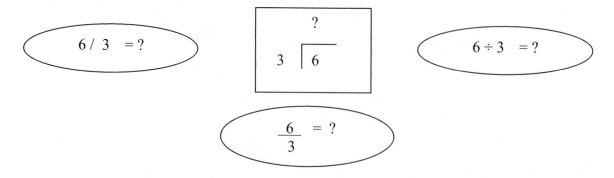

When performing long division, it is important to organize the information as is seen in the centre square. You have to understand how the different formats for division are transferred into the format seen above.

Example

$2653 \div 7 = ?$

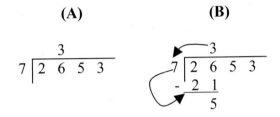

In order to answer a division question on paper, you must place the equation in the proper format. After this is accomplished you can begin to solve the problem.

(A)   **(B)**

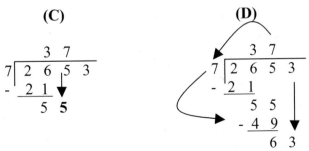

(A)

The first step is to focus on the highlighted area of the number under the bracket. You have to work with a number that is larger than the dividing number (7). Because 2 is smaller than 7, you have to work with 26. Ask yourself how many times you can multiply 7 without going over 26. If you count by 7's (7, 14, 21, 28) you'll realize that 3 is the most times that 7 will fit into 26.

(B)

With the information you have in section A, you now have to perform a simple multiplication. Take the top number (3) and multiply it by the dividing number (7). The answer is placed below 26 and then subtracted from the digits you were working with. (26 - 21 = 5) Make sure you keep the numbers in the proper columns. (If, after subtracting, the answer is greater than the dividing number, you need to start again using a larger top number.)

(C)   **(D)**

(C)

After subtraction, bring down the next digit to sit beside the solution. This becomes your new number to work with (55). Then repeat step A using this number. Determine how many times you can multiply 7 without exceeding 55. Place this digit above the next digit in the question on top of the bracket.

(D)

Next repeat step B. Multiply out the 7's and record your answer below the 55. Subtracting the numbers results in 6. Continue to work the same pattern, and bring down the next digit in the question to determine a new number to work with.

(E)

```
        3 7 9
   7 |2 6 5 3
     - 2 1
        5 5
      - 4 9
          6 3
        - 6 3
            0
```

(E)

The final steps in the process are to repeat the process. Determine how many times you can multiply 7 without going over 63. You can do this 9 times. When you multiply it out and subtract the result is 0. The answer to the question is shown above.

$$2653 \div 7 = 379$$

Decimals

There are times when you are dividing a number and, after the final subtraction, there is a value left over. This is a remainder. When this happens, you can choose whether or not to continue calculating the number. If you continue, 1 or more decimal points will be introduced.

Example:

```
        3 3 1                        3 3 1 . 6 2 5
    8 ⌐2 6 5 3                   8 ⌐2 6 5 3 . 0 0 0
     - 2 4                          - 2 4
         2 5                            2 5
       - 2 4                          - 2 4
           1 3                            1 3
         - 0 8                          - 0 8
             5                              5 0
                                         - 4 8
                                             2 0
                                           - 1 6
                                               4 0
                                             - 4 0
                                                 0
```

You must follow the same procedure with decimal places as you would with regular long division. Ensure that the digits are properly lined up, and continue adding 0's after the decimal places in the equation.

Decimals and Whole Numbers

You may be required to solve division problems with decimals already in place. Below are two examples of decimals occurring in division questions.

Example 1

```
                                    7 . 1 7
    5 ⌐3 5 . 8 5                5 ⌐3 5 . 8 5
```

To answer the question correctly, you have to place the decimal point in the answer directly above the decimal point in the question.

Example 2

```
                                     1 0 6 0 . 0
    2 . 7 ⌐2 8 6 2             27 ⌐2 8 6 2 0 . 0
```

When a decimal point is found in the denominator (the number of parts into which the whole is divided – bottom number of a fraction), then you must eliminate it before answering the question. This is achieved by shifting the decimal point however many spaces to the right it takes to create a whole number, in this example one space. This has to be matched by shifting the decimal place in the numerator (the number to be divided – top number of a fraction) by one space as well. If the numerator is a whole number, shift the decimal point right by adding a zero, as in the example above.

Example 3

$$3.5 \overline{)46.55} \qquad 35 \overline{)465.5} = 13.3$$

When a decimal point is found in both the numerator and the denominator you must combine both steps. First, you must eliminate the decimal place in the denominator, as in example 2. Then you have to ensure that the new decimal place lines up, as in example 1.

Hints

Long division becomes more complicated with higher numbers, especially higher denominators.

$$67 \overline{)3015} = 0045$$
$$\begin{array}{r} -268 \\ \hline 335 \\ -335 \\ \hline 0 \end{array}$$

Using 0's to Line up Numbers

67 will not fit into 3, or 30. You will therefore have to work with 301. By placing 0's above the 3 and the 0, (highlighted), you will not make any errors with improperly aligned numbers.

Rounding Up

Determining how many times 67 will fit into 301 can be a difficult task. It may help to round 67 up to 70. By counting 70 four times, you will reach 280. Five times equals 350, which exceeds 301. Four is the best guess, and by multiplying it out, using 67 you are proven correct.

Disregarding Decimals

The majority of the answers on a test will not require decimals. If your calculation of an equation gives you an answer with decimals, but none of the optional answers have decimals, stop calculating. Make a selection from the available options, or consider that you made a mistake. Quickly check your work, but don't spend too much time on one question that's causing you problems. Move onto the next question.

Zeros and Ones

Any time zero is divided by any other number the answer is 0.

$0 / 3 = 0$ $0 \div 25 = 0$ $\dfrac{0}{99} = 0$ $0 \overline{\smash{)}\,99}^{\,0}$

It is impossible for a number to be divided by 0. It is indefinable.

$9 / 0 = \text{undefined}$ $77 \div 0 = \text{undefined}$ $\dfrac{66}{0} = \text{undefined}$

Any number divided by 1 is equal to itself.

$3 / 1 = 3$ $55 \div 1 = 55$ $\dfrac{1,297}{1} = 1,297$ $1 \overline{\smash{)}\,38}^{\,38}$

Place Value

It is important to maintain proper place value of digits when performing mathematical calculations. You must be able to convert written numbers into digits. For example:

Two million, forty thousand and two	2,040,002
One and a half million	1,500,000
Ten thousand and ten	10,010

You can practice place value questions by answering questions such as the ones below:

a) Write a number that is 100 more than 4, 904.
b) Write a number that is 1000 less than 478, 243.
c) What number is one more than 9,999?
d) What is the value of 5 in the number 241, 598?
e) What figure is in the ten thousands place in 4,365,243?
f) What number is 30,000 less than 423,599?

The answers are listed below.

Place value is important when lining up numbers for addition and subtraction questions. For example:

$$15 + 1043 + 603 + 20,602 =$$

$$\begin{array}{r} 20,602 \\ 1,043 \\ 603 \\ \underline{15} \\ 22,263 \end{array}$$

$$13.09 + 0.4 + 206 + 0.002 =$$

$$\begin{array}{r} 206.000 \\ 13.090 \\ 0.400 \\ \underline{0.002} \\ 219.492 \end{array}$$

One of the most common errors is failing to place digits correctly under one another, which often occurs when trying to calculate these problems in your head.

Answers to practice questions.

a) 5,004   b) 477,243

c) 10,000   d) 500

e) 6   f) 393,599

Make sure you are comfortable with the proper names for the location of digits in a number.

1, 234, 567.890

1 = millions column

2 = hundred thousands column

3 = ten thousands column

4 = thousands column

5 = hundreds column

6 = tens column

7 = ones column

8 = tenths column

9 = hundredths column

0 = thousandths column

Order of Operations

The following rules have to be obeyed while working with mathematical equations. There is an order to how numbers are manipulated and worked on.

B E D M A S

You should memorize this acronym, as it tells you how to proceed with an equation.

1)   **B** – Brackets

        You must perform all mathematical calculations that occur within brackets before any other calculation in the equation.

2)   **E** – Exponents

        After calculations within brackets are handled, you have to perform any calculations with exponents next.

3)   **D / M** – Division and Multiplication

        Division and multiplication components are next. These are handled in the order they appear reading from left to right.

4)   **A / S** – Addition and Subtraction

        The final calculations are individual addition and subtraction questions, which are performed in the order they appear reading from left to right.

The best way to understand this process is to work through several problems.

Example 1:		
$6 + 5 \times 3 - 7$	Step 1: Multiplication	$5 \times 3 = 15$
$6 + 15 - 7$	Step 2: Addition	$6 + 15 = 21$
$21 - 7$	Step 3: Subtraction	$21 - 7 = 14$
Example 2:		
$14 - 7 + 18 \div 3$	Step 1: Division	$18 \div 3 = 6$
$14 - 7 + 6$	Step 2: Subtraction	$14 - 7 = 7$
$7 + 6$	Step 3: Addition	$7 + 6 = 13$

Example 3:

$7 + (15 - 6 \times 2)$	Step 1: Brackets Remember to follow the order of operation within the brackets. (Multiply before subtracting.)	$6 \times 2 = 12$
$7 + (15 - 12)$		$15 - 12 = 3$
$7 + 3$	Step 2: Addition	$7 + 3 = 10$

Example 4:

$2 (2 + 5)^2$	Step 1: Brackets	$2 + 5 = 7$
$2 (7)^2$	Step 2: Exponents	$7^2 = 7 \times 7 = 49$
$2 (49)$	Step 3: Multiplication	$2 \times 49 = 98$

Remember that two numbers separated only by brackets are multiplied together (a bracket = x.) $2 (6) = 6 \times 2$

Practice Questions

Try these practice questions to see if you are comfortable with mathematical order of operation. The final answers are listed below.

a) $7 - 4 + 6 \times 8 \div 2$

b) $14 + 8 (6 - 3)$

c) $30 - 3(5 - 2)^2$

d) $(5 - 1) (4 + 7)$

e) $75 - (6 \div (2+1))^2$

f) $10^2 - 10 + 3^2$

g) $(10 + 3) \times 2 + 6(5-2)$

h) $17 + 6^2 (18 \div 9)$

i) $4 (5+2-3+6)$

j) $10 (6 + (15 - (10-5)))$

Answers

a) 27

b) 38

c) 3

d) 44

e) 71

f) 99

g) 44

h) 89

i) 40

j) 160

Grouping Like Terms

You will come across mathematical problems where you have to group like terms together. Examples of this are very common with money. Whenever you are adding sums of money, there is no need to continually restate the same denominations. Below is an example of an equation adding up a suspect's money:

Denomination	# of Bills
$50	4
$20	3
$10	4

One means of calculating the total value of money seized is to individually add up all of the bills.

$$50 + 50 + 50 + 50 + 20 + 20 + 20 + 10 + 10 + 10 + 10$$

However, there is an easier and more orderly way of writing and working with this equation. Here is the statement rewritten separating the like terms.

$$(50 + 50 + 50 + 50) + (20 + 20 + 20) + (10 + 10 + 10 + 10)$$

Instead of adding all of the $50 bills together you can count the number of 50's and multiply that number by the value.

$50 + 50 + 50 + 50$	=	4 x 50 or 4 (50)
$20 + 20 + 20$	=	3 x 20 or 3 (20)
$10 + 10 + 10 + 10$	=	4 x 10 or 4 (10)

The statement can then be written more clearly as: $4(50) + 3 (20) + 4 (10)$

Remember that it doesn't matter what order the terms are in, so long as they remain together. The above equation could be restated any of the following ways:

$3(20) + 4(50) + 4(10)$ $20(3) + 50(4) + 10(4)$

$20(3) + 10(4) + 50(4)$ $4(10) + 3(20) + 4(50)$

Like terms can occur in any addition question. It doesn't have to be a monetary question. Any time you see two or more of the same number in an addition problem, they can be combined.

$5 + 6 + 3 + 5 + 2 + 6 + 5$	=	$3(5) + 2(6) + 3 + 2$
$75 + 63 + 75 + 63 + 75$	=	$3(75) + 2(63)$
$5 + 5 + 5 + 5 + 5 + 4$	=	$5(5) + 4$

Fractions

A fraction is simply a part of a whole thing. The example below is of a circle divided into four pieces. Each segment represents ¼ of the circle.

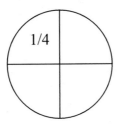

In each of the circles below, the same area is represented, but the area is divided into different numbers of equal parts.

1 / 2 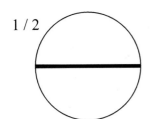   2 / 4 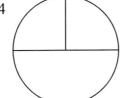   4 / 8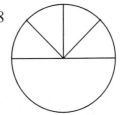

This diagram demonstrates that the fractions 1/2, 2/4 and 4/8 represent the same quantity.

1 / 3   2 / 6   3 / 9

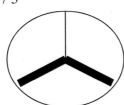  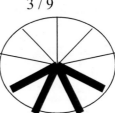

The fractions 1/3, 2/6 and 3/9 are equivalent. You can determine fractions of equivalent value by multiplying both the numerator and the denominator of the fraction by the same number.

$$\frac{1 \times 7}{3 \times 7} = \frac{7}{21} \qquad \text{thus} \qquad \frac{7}{21} = \frac{1}{3}$$

A similar rule holds when dividing the numerators and denominators of fractions. This is necessary to reduce fractions to their lowest form.

$$\frac{5 \text{ divided by } 5}{15 \text{ divided by } 5} = \frac{1}{3}$$

Improper Fractions

When a fraction has a larger numerator than denominator then the fraction is larger than one. The diagram below illustrates an example of improper fractions.

3 / 2 = 1 1/2

Adding and Subtracting Fractions

Whenever you are adding or subtracting fractions, you have to ensure that the denominators of the fractions are the same. For example:

$\frac{1}{2}$ + $\frac{6}{8}$ does not equal $\frac{7}{10}$

By multiplying both the denominator and the numerator of 1/2 by 4, you will be able to add the fractions together. 1 / 2 becomes 4 / 8.

$\frac{4}{8}$ + $\frac{6}{8}$ = $\frac{10}{8}$ = $\frac{5}{4}$

When you are adding and subtracting fractions, you also maintain the same denominator, and add or subtract the numerator.

$\frac{3}{4}$ - $\frac{1}{4}$ = $\frac{2}{4}$ = $\frac{1}{2}$ $\frac{3}{18}$ + $\frac{12}{18}$ = $\frac{15}{18}$ = $\frac{5}{6}$

$\frac{5}{10}$ - $\frac{3}{10}$ = $\frac{2}{10}$ = $\frac{1}{5}$ $\frac{7}{8}$ + $\frac{5}{8}$ = $\frac{12}{8}$ = $1\frac{1}{2}$

Multiplying Fractions

When multiplying fractions, there is no need to find a common denominator. Simply multiply the two top numbers and then multiply the two bottom numbers. Multiplying two fractions together (other than improper) will result in a fraction that is smaller than the original numbers.

$\frac{4}{5}$ x $\frac{3}{4}$ = $\frac{12}{20}$ = $\frac{3}{5}$ $\frac{1}{2}$ x $\frac{1}{5}$ = $\frac{1}{10}$

$\frac{3}{4}$ x $\frac{7}{18}$ = $\frac{21}{72}$ = $\frac{7}{24}$ $\frac{3}{2}$ x $\frac{4}{5}$ = $\frac{12}{10}$ = $1\frac{1}{5}$

Dividing Fractions

Division with fractions is very similar to multiplying with fractions.

12 divided by 12 = 1	12 goes into 12 once
12 divided by 6 = 2	6 goes into 12 twice
12 divided by 4 = 3	4 goes into 12 three times
12 divided by 3 = 4	3 goes into 12 four times
12 divided by 2 = 6	2 goes into 12 six times
12 divided by 1 = 12	1 goes into 12 twelve times
12 divided by 1/2 = 24	1/2 goes into 12 twenty four times

This is logical when you think about the statement on the right. Whenever you are dividing by a fraction you have to multiply one fraction by the reciprocal of the other. That is, when you divide one fraction by another, you have to multiply one fraction by the inverse of the other. For example:

$$\frac{1}{2} \div \frac{6}{7} = \frac{1}{2} \times \frac{7}{6} = \frac{7}{12}$$

$$\frac{3}{4} \div \frac{4}{5} = \frac{3}{4} \times \frac{5}{4} = \frac{15}{16}$$

$$1\frac{3}{4} \div \frac{4}{5} = \frac{7}{4} \times \frac{5}{4} = \frac{35}{16} = 2\frac{3}{16}$$

Whenever dividing mixed fractions (1 1/2, 2 3/4 etc) you must use improper fractions (3/2, 11/4 etc).

Percentages

It is important to have a solid background in decimals and fractions before you try to handle percentage questions. Percentages are simply fractions. Per means "out of" and cent means "a hundred". Percentages are fractions with 100 as a denominator. They are often noted with this sign: %.

10 % means 10 out of 100 or $\dfrac{10}{100}$

13 % means 13 out of 100 or $\dfrac{13}{100}$

100 % means 100 out of 100 or $\dfrac{100}{100}$

100% means everything. 100% of your salary is your whole salary. You simply follow the same rules of conversion from fractions to decimals for calculating percentages. Simply move the decimal points two places to the left to convert percents to decimals. This is essentially dividing the percentage by 100.

Example:

$75\% = 0.75$

$8\% = 0.08$

$53.5\% = 0.535$

$208\% = 2.08$

Any percent larger than 100% indicates more than the whole. For example:

A man's stock portfolio is worth 125% of what it was a year ago. This means that the stocks are now worth 25% more. If his stocks were worth $500 last year, they would be worth:

$500 x 125% =
$$\begin{array}{r} 500 \\ \times\ 1.25 \\ \hline \$\ 625 \end{array}$$

Percentages with Fractions

Some questions you encounter may incorporate percentages and fractions. Examples include 2 1/2 % or 33 1/3 %. In order to deal with these problems, you must first convert the percentages to improper fractions.

$$2\ 1/2 = 5/2 \qquad\qquad 33\ 1/3 = 100/3$$

After this step you simply carry out the division question.

```
      2 . 5              3 3 . 3 3
   2 ⌐5 . 0           3 ⌐1 0 0 . 0 0
     4
    ---
    1 0
    1 0
    ---
      0
```

Once you have the decimal equivalent of the percentage, you then follow the same rules that apply to a regular percentage. Divide the number by 100 or, more simply, move the decimal to the left twice. Thus:

$$2\ 1/2\% = 0.025 \qquad\qquad 33\ 1/3\% = 0.3333$$

Percentages You Should Memorize

25%	=	1 / 4	=	0.25
50%	=	1 / 2	=	0.5
75%	=	3 / 4	=	0.75
100%	=	4 / 4	=	1.00
33 1/3 %	=	1 / 3	=	0.333
66 2/3 %	=	2 / 3	=	0.666
10%	=	1 / 10	=	0.1
20%	=	1 / 5	=	0.2
40%	=	2 / 5	=	0.4
60%	=	3 / 5	=	0.6
80%	=	4 / 5	=	0.8

Decimal / Fraction Conversion Instruction

Fraction to Decimal

There are many situations where you will have to convert fractions to decimals. Decimals are often easier to work with. Changing fractions to decimals is simply a division problem. All you have to do is take the numerator and divide it by the denominator.

Examples:

$$1/2 = 2 \overline{\smash{)}\begin{array}{r} 0.5 \\ 1.0 \\ -1.0 \\ \hline 0 \end{array}}$$

$$4/5 = 5 \overline{\smash{)}\begin{array}{r} 0.8 \\ 4.0 \end{array}}$$

$$1/3 = 3 \overline{\smash{)}\begin{array}{r} 0.333 \\ 1.000 \\ -0.9 \\ \hline 0.10 \\ -09 \\ \hline 010 \\ -09 \\ \hline 1 \end{array}}$$

Mixed Fractions

Mixed fractions have to first be converted to improper fractions before they can be converted to decimals. Multiplying the whole number by the denominator and adding the numerator will achieve this. As soon as the improper fraction is found, you calculate the decimal in the same way as above.

Example 1

$$3 \frac{1}{2} = \frac{7}{2} \qquad 2 \overline{\smash{)}\begin{array}{r} 3.5 \\ 7.0 \end{array}}$$

Multiply 3 by 2, and then add 1. This is the new numerator, and the denominator remains the same.

Example 2

$$2 \frac{5}{6} = \frac{17}{6} \qquad 6 \overline{\smash{)}\begin{array}{r} 2.833 \\ 17.000 \end{array}}$$

Decimal to Fraction

When converting decimals to fractions, place value is extremely important. The first decimal point to the right of the decimal point is the tenths, followed by the hundredths, thousandths, etc. All you have to do is properly line up the place value with the proper denominator.

$$0.1 \quad \text{is a way of writing} \quad \frac{1}{10}$$

$$0.01 \quad \text{is a way of writing} \quad \frac{1}{100}$$

and

$$0.6 \quad \text{is a way of writing} \quad \frac{6}{10}$$

$$0.78 \quad \text{is a way of writing} \quad \frac{78}{100}$$

There is one zero in the denominator for every place to the right of the period in the original decimal.

Exponents

Exponents indicate how many times a number should be multiplied by itself. If a number is raised to the power of 2, the number should be multiplied by itself twice. If the number is raised to the power of 6, the number should be multiplied by itself 6 times.

$$2^2 = 2 \times 2 = 4$$

$$2^3 = 2 \times 2 \times 2 = 8$$

$$2^4 = 2 \times 2 \times 2 \times 2 = 16$$

$$2^5 = 2 \times 2 \times 2 \times 2 \times 2 = 32$$

$$7^2 = 7 \times 7 = 49$$

$$5^4 = 5 \times 5 \times 5 \times 5 = 625$$

Positive and Negative Integers

You must have an understanding of positive and negative integers and how they react when they are added, subtracted, multiplied and divided by each other. Look at the number line below. Positive integers exist to the right of the zero and negative integers exist to the left of the zero.

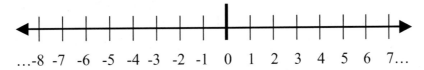

...-8 -7 -6 -5 -4 -3 -2 -1 0 1 2 3 4 5 6 7...

Adding Positive and Negative Integers

1) - 7 + 5 = -2   2) - 6 + 3 = -3
3) - 2 + 7 = 5   4) - 4 + 11 = 7

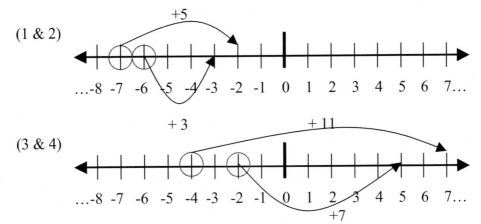

Subtracting Positive and Negative Integers

1) - 2 – 5 = -7   2) - 4 – 8 = -12
3) 4 – 7 = -3   4) 2 – 5 = -3

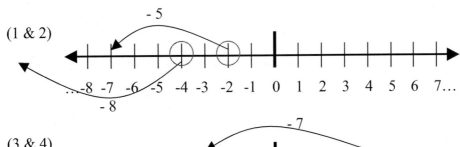

When adding and subtracting positive and negative integers you must know what to do when two signs are directly beside each other.

2 Positives	**2 Negatives**	**Opposite Signs**
+ + = +	- - = +	+ - = -

For instance:

	6 + (+3)	6 + (-3)	6 - (-3)
	= 6 + 3	= 6 – 3	= 6 + 3
	= 9	= 3	= 9

Try these sample questions. The answers are below.

1) 5 – 9 =   2) – 4 + 6 =   3) – 5 – 2 =   4) 2 – 7 =

5) –2 + 5 =   6) 1 – 9 =   7) 4 – (+6) =   8) –2 –(-4) =

9) + 3 – (-6) =   10) 6 + (-4) =   11) 6 + (+2) =   12) -3 + (-2) =

Multiplying and Dividing Positive and Negative Integers

While multiplying and dividing positive and negative integers, remember the rules that apply to adding and subtracting integers with two signs directly beside each other.

2 Positives	**2 Negatives**	**Opposite Signs**
+ + = +	- - = +	+ - = -

You should break questions like this into two steps.

Step 1: Solve the equation ignoring the signs.

6 x (-3) = 18	- 5 x 4 = 20
5 x (-7) = 35	- 3 x (-4) = 12
-12 ÷ (-4) = 3	-21 ÷ 3 = 7
36 ÷ (-9) = 4	-64 ÷ (-8) = 8

If you ignored the + and – signs in front of the numbers you would end up with the answers above.

Step 2: Determine the + / - sign. The rules about + / - integers come into play. If there are two + signs, then the equation is positive. If there are two − signs, then the equation is also positive. If there is one + and one − sign, then the equation is negative.

$$6 \times (-3) = \mathbf{-18} \quad (+ / -)$$
$$5 \times (-7) = \mathbf{-35} \quad (- / +)$$
$$-12 \div (-4) = \mathbf{3} \quad (- / -)$$
$$36 \div (-9) = \mathbf{-4} \quad (+ / -)$$

$$-5 \times 4 = \mathbf{-20} \quad (- / +)$$
$$-3 \times (-4) = \mathbf{12} \quad (- / -)$$
$$-21 \div 3 = \mathbf{-7} \quad (- / +)$$
$$-64 \div (-8) = \mathbf{8} \quad (- / -)$$

The final answers are displayed in bold above.

Try these sample questions. The answers are posted below.

a) $3 \times (-6) =$ b) $-2 \times (-9) =$ c) $-18 \div (-9) =$

d) $7 \times 7 =$ e) $-72 \div 8 =$ f) $-12 \times (-9) =$

g) $7 \times (-6) =$ h) $-28 \div (-4) =$ i) $16 \div (-4) =$

j) $3 \times (-4) =$ k) $-45 \div (-15) =$ l) $-3 \times (2) =$

Answers to Sample Questions

1) $5 - 9 = \mathbf{-4}$ 2) $-4 + 6 = \mathbf{2}$ 3) $-5 - 2 = \mathbf{-7}$

4) $2 - 7 = \mathbf{-5}$ 5) $-2 + 5 = \mathbf{3}$ 6) $1 - 9 = \mathbf{-8}$

7) $4 - (+6) = \mathbf{-2}$ 8) $-2 - (-4) = \mathbf{2}$ 9) $+3 - (-6) = \mathbf{9}$

10) $6 + (-4) = \mathbf{2}$ 11) $6 + (+2) = \mathbf{8}$ 12) $-3 + (-2) = \mathbf{-5}$

---

a) $3 \times (-6) = \mathbf{-18}$ b) $-2 \times (-9) = \mathbf{18}$ c) $-18 \div (-9) = \mathbf{2}$

d) $7 \times 7 = \mathbf{49}$ e) $-72 \div 8 = \mathbf{-9}$ f) $-12 \times (-9) = \mathbf{108}$

g) $7 \times (-6) = \mathbf{-42}$ h) $-28 \div (-4) = \mathbf{7}$ i) $16 \div (-4) = \mathbf{-4}$

j) $3 \times (-4) = \mathbf{-12}$ k) $-45 \div (-15) = \mathbf{3}$ l) $-3 \times (2) = \mathbf{-6}$

Perimeters

Perimeter is defined as the border around an object, or the outside edge of an object.

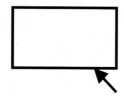

Perimeter is calculated by adding the sides of the object together.

Perimeter = 6 + 5 + 5 + 5 + 5 + 6
= 32

$$\begin{array}{c} 4 \\ 4 \quad \square \quad 4 \\ 4 \end{array}$$

Perimeter = 4 + 4 + 4 + 4
= 16

$$\begin{array}{c} 3 \quad 4 \\ 3 \end{array}$$

Perimeter = 3 + 3 + 4
= 10

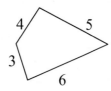

Perimeter = 3 + 4 + 5 + 6
= 18

Circumferences

Circumference is also defined as the border around a shape, but is always associated with a circle.

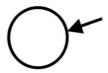

In order to determine the circumference of a circle, you must use a formula. You need to be familiar with some definitions.

$$\pi = 3.14 \text{ (pi)}$$

You are going to have to remember that pi is equal to 3.14.

Diameter (d)

Diameter is the distance from one edge of the circle, through the middle, to the opposite side of the circle.

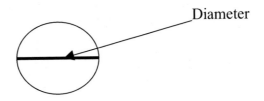

Radius (r)

Radius is defined as ½ of the diameter, or the distance from the mid-point of a circle to its outer edge.

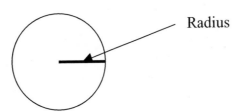

Formula for Calculating Circumference

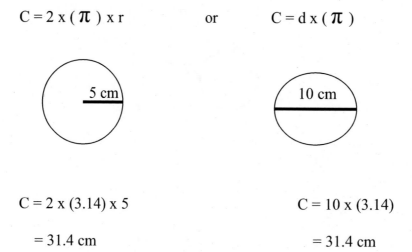

$$C = 2 \times (\pi) \times r \qquad \text{or} \qquad C = d \times (\pi)$$

$$C = 2 \times (3.14) \times 5 \qquad\qquad C = 10 \times (3.14)$$

$$= 31.4 \text{ cm} \qquad\qquad\qquad = 31.4 \text{ cm}$$

The information you are given in a question will dictate the formula you should use to calculate the circumference. If you are given the radius, calculate the diameter by multiplying by two. Dividing the diameter by two will give you the radius.

Areas

Area is space that is occupied within the borders of a shape. It is measured in units squared and is represented by the area shaded in the shapes below.

The three shapes you should know how to calculate area for are the triangle, rectangle and circle.

Area of a Rectangle or Square

To calculate the area of a square or rectangle, multiply the base of the object by its' height.

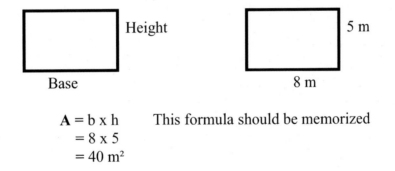

A = b x h   This formula should be memorized
  = 8 x 5
  = 40 m²

Area of a Triangle

To calculate the area of a triangle, follow the formula below.

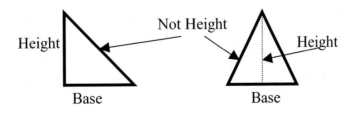

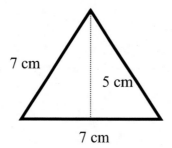

A = ½ x b x h   **This formula should be memorized.**
= ½ x 7 x 5
= 17.5 cm ^{2}

Remember that height is not necessarily an edge of the triangle, but the distance from the base to the top of the triangle.

Area of a Circle

To calculate the area of a circle, follow the formula below.

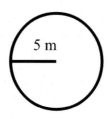

A = π (r) ^{2} **This formula should be memorized.**
= (3.14) (5) ^{2}
= (3.14) (25)
= 78.5 m ^{2}

Other Shapes

You may have to calculate the area of shapes other than basic squares, triangles and circles. You can attempt to break shapes into smaller components and use the formulas above. For example:

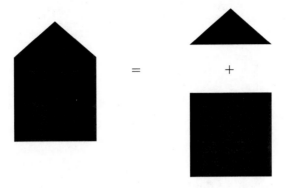

Calculate the area of the triangle and adding it to the area of the square results in the area of the whole shape.

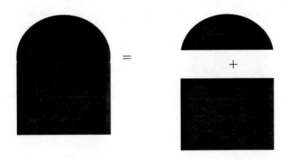

You can divide the shape on the left into a square and a half circle. Calculate the area of the square and the area of the circle. Divide the area of the circle in half and add the two together.

Volumes

Volume is defined as the area occupied by a three dimensional shape. If you pictured an empty cup, volume is the amount of liquid it contains. Calculating volume for different objects can be very difficult and involves complex formulas. We will discuss how to calculate the volume of three simple objects. Volume is always discussed in units cubed (example 3m^3.)

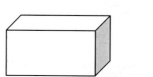

Volume of a Cube

You should memorize the formula for calculating the volume of a cube.

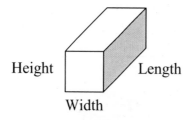 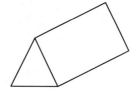

Height   Length   4 m   6 m

Width   4 m

V = length x width x height
= 6 x 4 x 4
= 96 m ^{3}

Volume of a Cylinder

To calculate the volume of a cylinder, determine the area of the circle and multiply it by the height of the cylinder.

Radius = 5 m

Height = 10 m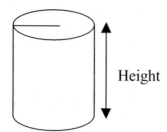

Height

$V = \pi\ (r)^2$ x height
= (3.14) (5)^2 (10)
= 785 m ^{3}

Volume of a Triangular Shaped Object

To calculate the volume of an object like the one below, first calculate the area of the triangle and multiply it by the height of the object.

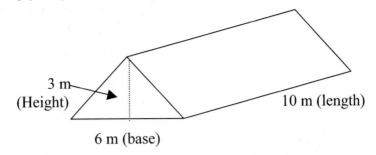

3 m
(Height)

10 m (length)

6 m (base)

$$V = \frac{1}{2} \text{ (base) (height) (length)}$$
$$= \frac{1}{2} (6) (3) (10)$$
$$= 90 \text{ m}^3$$

Metric Conversions

The key to understanding metric conversions is to memorize the prefixes and roots to each word. The root of each word indicates the basic measurement (litre, metre, gram), while the prefixes determine the relative size of the measurement (larger or smaller units – milli, centi, kilo, etc,).

Prefixes

All units in the metric system are easily converted because they are all based on units of 10. When converting between different measurements of the same base unit, it is as easy as shifting the decimal point.

For example:

432,000 millimetres
43,200 centimetres   ALL EQUAL EACH OTHER
432 metres
0.432 kilometres

Length

Length is used to measure the distance between points. The base unit for length is the metre. The most common units you'll encounter with length include:

Millimetres – small units (25 millimetres in 1 inch)
Centimetres – small units (2.5 centimetres in 1 inch)
Metres – larger units (1 metre = 3.2 feet or 1.1 yards)
Kilometres – large units (1.6 kilometres in 1 mile)

Prefix	Example	Sign	Conversion
Milli	Millimetres	mm	1 m = 1000 mm
Centi	Centimetre	cm	1 m = 100 cm
Deca	Decagram	dm	1 m = 10 dm
-	Metre	m	1 m = 1 m
Kilo	Kilometre	km	1 km = 1000 m

Volume

Volume is defined as the capacity of a given container. It usually measures the amount of liquid or gas that an object can hold. For example, the volume of a pop can is 355 millilitres, or the volume of a milk carton is 1 litre. The base unit for volume in the metric system is the litre. A litre is roughly the amount of milk that will fit into a milk carton or roughly three glasses of milk.

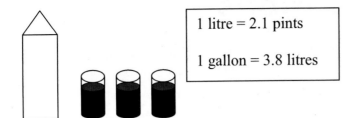

1 litre = 2.1 pints

1 gallon = 3.8 litres

The most common prefix used with volume is the millilitre (used to measure small amounts, such as tablespoons.) The majority of the time when measuring volume you will be using the litre measurement itself.

Prefix	Example	Sign	Conversion
Milli	Millilitres	mL	1 L = 1000 mL
Centi	Centilitres	cL	1 L = 100 cL
Deca	Decalitres	dL	1 L = 10 dL
-	Litres	L	1 L = 1 L
Kilo	Kilolitres	kL	1 kL = 1000 L

Mass or Weight

The base unit for weight in the metric system is the gram. The most common units you'll encounter with weight are:

Milligrams – very small (1000 milligrams in 1 gram)
Grams – small units (28.3 grams in 1 ounce)
Kilograms – large units (1 kilogram = 2.2 pounds)

Prefix	Example	Sign	Conversion
Milli	Milligrams	mg	1 g = 1000 mg
Centi	Centigram	cg	1 g = 100 cg
Deca	Decagram	dg	1 g = 10 dg
-	Gram	G	1 g = 1 g
Kilo	Kilogram	kg	1 kg = 1000 g

Algebraic Equations

Before beginning this section, make sure that you are comfortable with the rules of order of operation in mathematical equations. It is necessary to know in what order you add, subtract, divide and multiply in an equation.

Algebraic equations involve using letters and symbols to represent unknown numbers. In order to solve these equations you must isolate the unknown variable. We will begin with a couple of simple examples.

When solving algebraic equations, it is important to know the opposite mathematical operations. For example, subtraction is the opposite of addition and division is the opposite of multiplication. Square roots are the opposite of squaring. We will not cover square roots in this section.

$6 + y = 12$

$6 + y - 6 = 12 - 6$

$y = 6$

> In order to isolate the "y", eliminate a + 6 on the left hand side of the equation. In algebraic equations, whatever you do to one side of the equation you must also do to the other side. Subtract 6 from both sides.

$y - 3 = 15$

$y - 3 + 3 = 15 + 3$

$y = 18$

> In order to isolate the "y", eliminate a - 3 on the left hand side of the equation. Add 3 to both sides.

$7y = 42$

$7y / 7 = 42 / 7$

$y = 6$

> In this case, "y" is multiplied by 7. To eliminate a number that is being multiplied, divide by the same number. Divide both sides by 7.

$y / 12 = 5$

$y / 12 \times 12 = 5 \times 12$

$y = 60$

> In this case, "y" is divided by 12. To eliminate a number that is being divided, multiply by the same number. Multiply both sides by 12.

Practice solving some of these simple equations:

1) $y / 11 = 23$ 2) $15 + y = 63$ 3) $-5 + y = 10$

4) $13 (y) = 130$ 5) $5 y = 15$ 6) $6 + 3 + y = 56$

7) $2(y) = 56$ 8) $y / 8 = 4$ 9) $y (24) = 72$

Answers are below.

More Advanced Algebraic Equations

When solving equations, follow the order of operations which dictate that you perform equations within brackets, followed by exponents, then division and multiplication, and finally addition and subtraction. When isolating unknown variables, use the opposite order. We will not cover solving equations with exponents at this level.

$6 y + 12 = 84$

$6 y + 12 - \mathbf{12} = 84 - \mathbf{12}$

$6 y = 72$

$6 y / \mathbf{6} = 72 / \mathbf{6}$

$y = 12$

> In order to isolate the "y", first eliminate a $+ 12$ on the left hand side of the equation. Subtract 12 from both sides. You are left with $6y = 12$.
> To isolate "y", now simply divide both sides of the equation by 6.

$y / 3 + 12 - 2 = \mathbf{15 \times 3} + 4$

$y / 3 + 12 - 2 = 45 + \mathbf{4}$

$y / 3 + 12 - 2 = 49$

$y / 3 + 12 - 2 + \mathbf{2} = 49 + \mathbf{2}$

$y / 3 + 12 = 51$

$y / 3 + 12 - \mathbf{12} = 51 - \mathbf{12}$

$y / 3 = 39$

$y / 3 \times \mathbf{3} = 39 \times \mathbf{3}$

$y = 117$

> You may encounter equations where one side has operations without an unknown variable. In cases like this, solve the side without an unknown variable FOLLOWING THE STANDARD ORDER OF OPERATION RULES.
>
> After you have accomplished this, solve the equation in the standard manner. People more advanced in math will be able to consolidate portions of the left side as well, but unless you are comfortable you should proceed the way outlined to the left.

$(6 - y) \times 3 = 24$

$(6 - y) \times 3 / \mathbf{3} = 24 / \mathbf{3}$

$(6 - y) = 8$

$6 - y - \mathbf{6} = 8 - \mathbf{6}$

$-y = 2$

$-y \times \mathbf{(-1)} = 2 \times \mathbf{(-1)}$

$y = -2$

Perform this equation following the standard rules. Leave the brackets until the end. When only the brackets remain, you can get rid of them as they no longer serve a purpose.

When you are left with an equation where the unknown is isolated, but negative, simply multiply both sides of the equation by -1 to inverse the signs.

The end result is that $y = -2$.

$18 / y = 2$

$18 / y \times \mathbf{(y)} = 2 \times \mathbf{(y)}$

$18 = 2y$

$18 / \mathbf{2} = 2y / \mathbf{2}$

$9 = y$

One other tricky situation you may encounter is when "y" appears on the bottom of a division equation. In order to solve for "y", move it from the bottom of the division sign by multiplying both sides of the equation by "y". The result is $18 = 2y$. Now solve the rest of the equation.

WHATEVER YOU DO TO ONE SIDE OF AN EQUATION YOU MUST ALSO DO TO THE OTHER SIDE.

More Practice Questions

a) $3(y) + 6 - 10 = 89$

b) $(y) / 6 + 24 - 2 = 14$

c) $-y(3) + 55 = 105$

d) $5y - 32 = 24(3)$

e) $-32 + 6y/2 = 64$

f) $22y + 16(8) = 6y$

Answers:

1) 253	2) 48	3) 15
4) 10	5) 3	6) 47
7) 28	8) 32	9) 3

a) 31	b) -48	c) -16.7
d) 20.8	e) 32	f) -8

Teaching Material
English

Common Grammar Errors

It is beyond the scope of this book to cover all grammar errors that can occur during a government examination. Below are merely some examples you may come across. If you feel your grammar is a significant barrier to landing the job, it would be prudent to review a grammar textbook, or perhaps take an English grammar course.

The Use of "Then" and "Than"

"Then" is used to indicate time. It has the same meaning as "afterwards", "subsequently" or "followed by".

>   Ex: I went to the play, ***and then*** I went home.

"Than" is used in comparison. It can be used with the word "rather". It has the same meaning as "as opposed to", or "instead of".

>   Ex: I would rather play baseball ***than*** hockey.

The Use of "Is When"

This is not correct. Use the term "occurs when."

>   Ex: The best part of the movie ***occurs when*** the killer is revealed.

Subordinate Clauses

Be careful with subordinate clauses. If one clause has less emphasis (less importance) in a sentence, it is subordinate or dependent on the other clause. When these clauses occur at the beginning of the sentence, they can be tricky.

>   Ex: ***Since you began training,*** you have been unable to work an entire shift.

If you rearrange the sentence you can understand how "since" acts as the conjunction.

>   Ex: You have been able to work an entire shift **since you began training.**

Forming Plurals

It is difficult to determine the plural form of many words. Examples include:

Goose	Geese	Man	Men
Woman	Women	Mouse	Mice
Mother-in-Law	Mothers-in-Law		

Comparative Adjectives and Adverbs

Single Syllable Words:

To form the comparative adjective or adverb for most single syllable words, add *"-er"* to the end of the word. If there are three or more parties to compare, use the ending *"-est."*

Rafik was strong.
Bill was *stronger* than Rafik.
Pratik was the *strongest* of the three.

Sean is fast.
Sean is the faster of the two.
Sean is the fastest of the three.

Be careful. There are always exceptions to the rule in the English language. You should be able to tell by the sound of the words when you should use an alternative method of comparison.

I had a fun time at the party this year.
I had *more fun* this year than last year.
I had the *most fun* this year compared to all the other parties.

The words "funner" and "funnest" do not exist.

Multiple Syllable Words:

As with the example "fun", multiple syllable words use linking words while making comparisons. When comparing two parties, use the word *"more"*; and while comparing three or more parties, use the word *"most"*.

He was *more eager* than her to finish the project.
He was the *most eager* of the three to finish the project.

Shelley was *more intelligent* than Michael.
Lucy was the *most intelligent* of the group.

Subject / Verb Agreement

It is important to make sure that the verb agrees with the noun it relates to. There are six types of persons in the English language:

I	We
You (singular)	You (plural)
He / She / It	They

In English, there are several ways that subjects and verbs relate to each other. Here are a couple:

I	*run / do / was*	We	*run / do / were*
You	*run / do / was*	You	*run / do / were*
He / She / It	*runs / does / was*	They	*run / do / were*

Be careful of confusing the subject and verb agreement.

Example: I run fast.   I do well.   I **don't** understand.
                   He runs fast.   He does well.   He **doesn't** understand.

This can be difficult if there is a clause between the subject and the verb. When analyzing a sentence, try to read the sentence without the clause to determine if there is subject / verb agreement.

Example: ***Dheena***, along with the rest of us, ***does*** well.
Read aloud: ***Dheena does well.*** "Dheena do well" doesn't sound right.

The Use of "It's" and "Its"

This is often wrongly expressed.
"It's" is a contraction that translates into "it is".

It's getting late. = ***It is*** getting late.
I'm tired and ***it's*** time to go. = I'm tired and ***it is*** time to go.

"Its" refers to possession. It is the equivalent to an apostrophe "s".

The train and all ***its*** passengers were safe.
The train and all **the train's** passengers were safe.

The Use of "There", "Their" and "They're"

These are also often confused. Here are the definitions:

There: a location, nearby, in attendance, present
          The book is over **there,** on the table.

Their: a possessive pronoun implying ownership, belonging to them,
          I took **their** advice and followed through with the job.

They're: a contraction, meaning "they are"
          They're going to arrive late because of the snow.

The Use of "Two", "To", and "Too"

Make sure you follow these definitions. Use the correct "to/too/two" in the proper place.

    <u>To</u>: in the direction, toward, near, in order to.
        I went **to** the store **to** buy some bread.

    <u>Too</u>: also, as well, in addition, besides, and excessively.
        The teacher handed out an "A" to Bill and to Cindy, **too.**
        Shayna and Jeff just left **too**.
        The pizza deliverer took **too** long, so the pizza was free.

    <u>Two</u>: the number
        There were **two** beavers sitting on the log.

Verb Tenses

When reading a passage, ensure that the verbs in a sentence agree and that verbs discussing the same idea are in the same tense. For example, if you are speaking in the past in one sentence, you must remain consistent in the sentence following.

    Incorrect
    Bill **ran** to the store very quickly. He **is taking** Sally with him.
    Sean **reads** at a fourth grade level and **studied** very hard.

    Correct:
    Bill **ran** to the store very quickly. He **took** Sally with him.
    Sean **reads** at a fourth grade level and **studies** very hard.

Adverbs and Adjectives

Adverbs are used to modify or compliment verbs, adjectives or other adverbs. They generally explain how (gently), when (soon), or where (fully). A common trait of adverbs is to end in "*-ly*". However, this is not a reliable way to tell adverbs and adjectives apart.

Adjectives are used with nouns to describe a quality or modify a meaning. (old, tall, curly, Canadian, my, this...)

If the word you are describing or modifying is a noun, make sure you use the adjective form of the word. If the word is a verb, adjective, or adverb, use the adverb format.

He ran **quickly** down the street.	- Adverb quickly (how he runs)
He was a very **quick** thinker.	- Adjective quick (describing the thinker)
It was a **very large** house.	- Adverb very (describing large)
	- Adjective large (describing house)

It was a **loud** song.   - Adjective loud (describing song)
She sang **loudly**.   - Adverb loudly (modifying sang)

Uses of Commas in Lists

When a list is presented in a sentence, use commas between list items and a conjunction to separate the last two items on the list. It is not wrong to add an additional comma before the conjunction, but it is unnecessary.

He was going to bring his **toys, clothes, books and cookies** to class.

Angela was going to the Maritimes by **plane, train or boat**.

Uses of the Apostrophe

Apostrophes are used to indicate ownership.

Bill's school was one of the best in the country. (the school to which Bill went)
Martha's mirror was cracked. (the mirror belonging to Martha)

Meanings of "Fair" and "Fare"

People often confuse these two words. Definitions are listed below.

Fair: just, reasonable, light, fair haired, pale

He was a **fair** judge and handed down reasonable sentences.
The boy was very **fair**, and would burn easily in the sun.

Fare: charge, price, ticket, tariff, passenger

The **fare** for the plane was rather steep.

Subject / Object Noun Agreements

Depending on its role in the sentence, pronouns take on different forms. Below is a list.

Subject		Object	
I	We	Me	Us
You	You	You	You
He / She / It	They	Him / Her / It	Them

If the pronoun is acting as a subject, use a subject pronoun.

Subject	**Object**
Tim and I went to the baseball game.	Tim threw the ball to me.
He was the last one to leave.	Shayna surprised her at the party.
They will come later.	Alex passes the gravy to them.

The major distinction between a subject and an object is the manner in which the verb relates to the pronouns. A subject tends to perform the verb, while an object tends to have the verb performed on it. Read the examples above and see if you understand the difference. If not, you will have to check with a grammar textbook.

Double Negatives

Avoid using double negatives when both speaking and writing,. Examples include:

I do **not** want **no** gum.	I do **not** want **any** gum.
You can**'t** go to **no** store.	You can**'t** go to **any** store.
The sergeant has**n't no** time.	The sergeant has**n't any** time.

The uses of "From" and "Off"

When receiving objects, goods or information, remember that the word "from" is correct even though in common spoken language we often use the word "off".

> The doctor received the X-rays **from** the technician.
> She pulled the book **from** the cupboard.

The Uses of "Stayed" and "Stood"

This is similar to the "From" and "Off" problem mentioned above. You often hear the word "stood" used in spoken language, but "stayed" is the correct word to use.

Stood is the past tense of stand (position, place, locate). Stayed is the past tense of stay (remain, wait, reside.)

> I should have stayed with my fellow officers in the tough times.
> The nurse stayed by the patient all night long.

The Use of Amount and Number

Generally speaking, we use "**amount**" with something that is measured or can't be counted, such as weights or volumes. We use "**number**" to describe quantities that are countable.

> She had a large **amount** of liquid in the test tube.
> There was a large **amount** of chocolate used in the recipe.
> There were a large **number** of soldiers in the army.
> The **number** of signs on the highway is enormous.

Run-On Sentences

Watch out for run-on sentences when writing. When two or more separate independent clauses are incorrectly joined, this is a run-on sentence. An independent clause is the part of a sentence that could stand alone. If you put a period at the end of an independent clause, it could serve as a sentence.

Here is an example of a run-on sentence:

Jamie was extremely angry when he missed his final chemistry exam, he went back to his dormitory and yelled at his roommate for failing to wake him up.

There are several ways to deal with a run-on sentence.

1) Make two Separate Sentences.

This is the easiest way to correct the problem. Simply add a period and start the second sentence with a capital letter.

> Correct:
> Jamie was extremely angry when he missed his final chemistry exam. He went back to his dormitory and yelled at his roommate for failing to wake him up.

2) Use a semicolon to separate the independent clauses.

Semicolons can often replace periods, but a comma can't. Do not capitalize the word immediately after a semicolon.

> Correct:
> Jamie was extremely angry when he missed his final chemistry exam; he went back to his dormitory and yelled at his roommate for failing to wake him up.

3) Use a subordinating conjunction with one of the clauses.

A subordinating conjunction is used to turn one of the clauses from an independent clause to a dependent clause. Examples of subordinating conjunctions include "because" and "since".

> Correct:
> Since Jamie was extremely angry when he missed his final chemistry exam, he went back to his dormitory and yelled at his roommate for failing to wake him up.

4) Use a comma and a coordinating conjunction between the two clauses.

Coordinating conjunctions can connect two clauses. The most common coordinating conjunctions include "and", "or", "but", and "so".

> Correct:
> Jamie was extremely angry when he missed his final chemistry exam, so he went back to his dormitory and yelled at his roommate for failing to wake him up.

5) Use a semicolon, conjunctive adverb and comma to separate the clauses.

Conjunctive adverbs can connect clauses. Examples of these adverbs include: "therefore", "moreover", "however", and "nonetheless". In order to properly use these adverbs, place a semicolon before the adverb and a comma after the adverb.

> Incorrect:
> Jamie was extremely angry when he missed his final chemistry exam, therefore he went back to his dormitory and yelled at his roommate for failing to wake him up.

> Correct:
> Jamie was extremely angry when he missed his final chemistry exam; therefore, he went back to his dormitory and yelled at his roommate for failing to wake him up.

Sentence Fragments

A sentence fragment is an incomplete sentence. There are two ways to change a sentence fragment to a complete sentence.

1) Add Words

Incorrect:
> Justin, running across the front lawn and enjoying his childhood days.
> (incomplete sentence)

Correct:
> Justin was running across the front lawn and enjoying his childhood days.
> (complete sentence)

2) Take Away Words

Creating a complete sentence from a sentence fragment can also be achieved by removing words from the sentence fragment.

Incorrect:
> While Trevor was completing the exam but having difficulty coming up with the answer to question #51.

Correct:
Trevor was completing the exam but having difficulty coming up with the answer to question #51.

Other Common Grammar Errors

Attend -	go to, be present at, concentrate
Tend -	be inclined, be likely, to have a tendency
Lose -	misplace, unable to find, to be defeated
Loose -	unfastened, wobbly, slack, movable
Threw -	hurled, tossed, past tense of "to throw"
Through -	from first to last, during, in the course of
Weather -	the seasons, elements, temperatures
Whether -	question of if, introducing an alternative possibility
Bear -	an animal in the woods, or to tolerate, stand, put up with
Bare -	to expose, naked, uncovered

Teaching Material
General

Observation and Memory

Memory

Developing your memory is a skill like any other, and will improve the more you practice. There are several methods to go about doing this.

1) Practice as many of the practice tests as possible to become familiar with the methods used during the real exam.
2) Practice reading passages and pictures in newspapers and magazines. Focus on names, and test yourself 30 minutes later to see how you did.
3) Have a friend note the makes, colours, and license plates of a few cars in an area and test yourself 30 minutes later.
4) Form pictures or links in your mind to assist your memory. For example, if you see a mug shot of a person that reminds you of your friend, link that friend to the mug shot in order to memorize it. Here is an example using license plates.

954 PNY	- remember 954 **P**eople in **N**ew **Y**ork
651 ZTZ	- remember 651 **Z**ee **T**ea**Z**e (the tease)
421 PLM	- remember 421 **PL**u**M**ber

Do whatever works for you. (Psychologists have found that by making expressions graphic, people remember them more easily.)

Observation

The observations and mapping questions are skills that can only be developed through repetitive practice. Tips to improve your observation skills include:

1) Take the practice exams in this book (or on the website) to become familiar with the testing process.

2) Purchase "spot the difference" puzzles.

3) Do word find puzzles in local papers.

4) Practice Mapping questions with friends using local maps, or building schematics.

Facial Visualization Questions

Facial visualization questions are common in entrance exams. They test your powers of observation and ability to spot similarities and differences between suspects that look alike. This is a necessary skill for a peace officer, as you will be asked to locate suspects with vague descriptions, or you may be dealing with an old photo or need to visualize what a suspect would look like with glasses, facial hair, etc.

Assume that the suspect's facial appearance has not changed in any permanent way. For example, a suspect might comb his or her hair differently, put on glasses, wear a different hat or grow facial hair. Any changes to bone structure, weight or facial features that would require plastic surgery should be excluded.

Which of the following four suspects matches the man shown above?

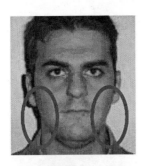

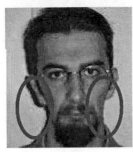

You should focus on areas of the face that are difficult to change. As the circles demonstrate in the first and third photos, there seems to be an inconsistency with the cheek structure and general shape of the jaw. The jaw is too wide in the first photo and too narrow in the third. The fourth photo is a close match but the nose is not the right shape.

Some of the tests will use actual photographs of suspects, while others will use cartoon drawings of suspects. The same principles apply. Focus on:

- Shape of the head
- Shape and placement of the eyes
- Shape of the nose

- Shape of the chin
- Shape of the cheeks

Try to overlook or disregard any easy changes that a suspect can make to his/her appearance, such as:

Change in hairstyle
Change in facial hair

Glasses
Hats

Jewellery

Eliminate as Many Choices as Possible, then Guess

You will not be penalized if you guess incorrectly in these tests. Because there is a time limit, you must be efficient and use your time optimally. Don't waste too much time on one question. Look at your four options, eliminate as many as possible, and then guess which of the remaining ones is best. Remember, the questions will get more difficult throughout the test, so expect to spend more time on later questions than on the earlier ones.

Judgement Section

Framework for Analysis

It is important to have a framework for how you will approach judgement questions during an examination process. You must know how to establish hierarchies in order to prioritize activities and handle conflicting job requirements. Below is a possible value hierarchy that can be used to resolve difficult decisions.

1) Protection of Life and Limb.
This is an officers' first priority and supersedes all other decisions. This includes the lives of officers as well.

2) Obeying Orders in Emergency Situations
Officers have to be able to follow instructions even though they may not fully understand the justification for them.

3) Protection of Property
This is a primary duty of officers.

4) Performing other Required Duties
Officers then must act as required to keep the peace, enforce the law, and maintain order.

Remember that while you are performing your duties, your priorities include:

1) Assisting Endangered People (including victims of crime, injured people, etc.)

2) Keeping the Peace (calming disorder, preventing destruction)

3) Enforcing the Law (fairly and impartially)

4) Maintaining Order (investigating suspicious events, working with community members, correcting traffic problems)

5) Assisting Others Who Need Help (disabled, children, elderly, etc.)

Core Competencies

Review the list of core competencies found in the resume section. Remember that officer safety is paramount.

Pattern Solving

When you are attempting to solve patterns, be very observant and look for consistent changes and developments. These changes can include, but are not exclusive to:

1) Number of objects
2) Size of objects
3) Colour of objects
4) Shape of objects
5) Rotation / Flip of objects
6) Number of unique identifying marks

There are a number of different clues you must look for. The only way to improve your skills for this stage of the exam is to practice the puzzles in this book, on the website or puzzle books you may find in bookstores.

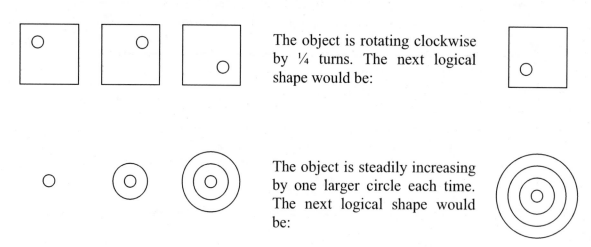

The object is rotating clockwise by ¼ turns. The next logical shape would be:

The object is steadily increasing by one larger circle each time. The next logical shape would be:

Sometimes you have to ignore information to detect the pattern.

You must ignore the shapes in this case. The image is increasing the number of highlighted objects one at a time (0, 1, 2, 3). The next logical shape would be:

Spelling Section

The following is a list of words that you should be able to spell.

ability	abundance	absence	absolute
acceleration	acceptable	accessory	accident
accidentally	accuracy	accused	achieved
achievement	acknowledge	acknowledgement	acquaintance
acquired	acquittal	activity	actual
addition	addressed	adequate	administration
admissible	adolescent	advancement	advice
advise	agency	agreement	aggressive
alcohol	alight	align	alleged
allegedly	allergy	alliance	allocate
allowed	alternative	amateur	ambitious
ambulance	analyse	anniversary	announcement
annual	anonymous	answered	anticipated
antique	anxieties	anxious	apologise
apology	appalling	apparent	appeal
appearance	appliance	applicant	argument
artificial	assistance	attachment	authorities
authority	awkward	backwards	balance
bandage	bankrupt	barrister	basis
beautiful	before	behaviour	beneficial
bicycle	blanket	blatant	blockage
blurred	boredom	borrowed	boundaries
breach	broken	breathing	broaden
building	buoyant	bureau	burglaries
calculated	calendar	camera	campaign
candidate	capability	capital	cardboard
career	careful	carriage	casualty
caught	cause	centre	certificate
changing	chaos	character	chemical
circumstances	citizen	civil	claimed
clause	clearance	climate	coincide
colleague	collection	collision	column
combination	comment	commencement	commercial
commission	commissioner	commitment	committee
communication	community	compatible	competent
composure	comprehend	condemned	condition
consequence	consideration	consistent	constant
controversial	controversy	convenient	corpse
corroborate	corruption	coughing	courage
courageous	courteous	cultural	credible
criminal	critical	criticism	crucial
daughter	debris	decentralise	decisive
defendant	demonstrate	denial	deposit

depth	descendant	description	despite
detailed	determined	detour	development
diagnose	diameter	diesel	difference
direction	disability	disappointing	disappointment
disappearance	discipline	discount	discretion
discussion	disguise	dishonest	disillusionment
dismissed	disqualified	distance	distinction
distinguish	distressed	distribute	disturbance
diversity	division	document	domestic
dominant	double	doubtful	draught
duplicate	durable	duration	effective
efficient	electricity	element	eligible
eliminate	embarrass	emergency	eminent
emphasis	employment	empty	encounter
endeavour	energetic	enforce	engagement
enjoyable	enormous	enough	enthusiasm
environment	equality	equation	equipment
equity	eruption	essential	ethnic
evasion	exaggerate	examination	exceed
excess	exception	exceptional	executive
expenses	facilities	fatigue	favourite
feature	February	festival	fictitious
fierce	financial	fixture	floating
flowing	fluorescent	focussed	foreign
foreseeable	forgiveness	formal	fortnight
foundation	fraudulent	frightened	front
fulfilment	function	furniture	gauge
generate	genuine	government	gracious
gradually	grasping	grateful	grievance
grievous	growth	guarantee	guard
guest	guidance	handkerchief	handle
harbour	harden	haste	hazard
headquarters	health	height	heroin
highway	history	holiday	homicide
honesty	honorary	humour	hypnotize
ideal	identification	identify	ignore
illegal	illegible	illusion	illustrate
imagination	imitate	immature	immediately
immensely	immigration	impact	impartial
implement	implication	important	improvement
improvise	impulsive	inaccurate	incapable
incident	inclination	inclusion	income
incorporate	incredible	incriminate	inconsiderate
independent	indicate	indigenous	indirect
individual	industrial	inferior	inflammable

inflation influence influential information
informative inheritance initial initiative
injection injuries innocent inspector
inspiration instalment instance instead
institution instrument insulate insurance
intangible integrate integrity intellectual
intelligent intend intensity intent
intercept interference interim intermittent
internal interpret interrupt view
intrigue introduction intrusion invasion
investigation invitation irrational irreconcilable
irresponsible irritate jealous jeopardy
journalist joyous judgement junior
juror justice justification juvenile
keyboard kilometre kitchen kneel
knocking knowledge knowledgeable known
labourer lacquer laminate language
laundry lawful leaflet league
legality legible legislation legitimate
leisure length leverage liberty
library licence licensing lighten
likelihood limb limited linear
lining liquidate liquor literally
literate litigation litre location
logical loose lose lunged
luxurious machinery magazine magnificent
maintenance malicious management manipulate
mannerism manslaughter marijuana marketing
marriage masculine massacre massive
material maturity maximum mayor
measurement mechanical mediate mediation
medicine mediocre memory merchandise
merge merit metropolitan microscope
middle military miniature minimum
minister mischievous misconduct miserable
missile mission mobile modern
module momentary monitored monopoly
monotonous monument motion mould
mourning movement multiply municipal
murmur muscle narcotic narrative
narrow nationality naïve natural
navigate nearby necessary necessitate
negotiable negotiation neighbour neighbourhood
nervous neutral niche noisy
nominate normally nothing novelty
nudged nuisance nurseries nurture
nutrition objective obligation obscenity
obscure observation obstacle obsolete

obtain	obviously	occasion	occupation
occurred	occurrence	offence	offender
offensive	official	omitted	onus
opening	operation	opinion	opponent
opportunity	opposite	opposition	optimistic
option	ordeal	ordered	ordinary
organisation	orientation	original	otherwise
ought	outcome	outlining	overall
overturn	pacify	paddle	painting
palm	panic	parade	paragraph
parallel	parliament	participate	particle
particularly	particular	partition	partner
passage	patient	patrol	pattern
pause	pavement	payment	peculiar
pedestrian	penalty	pensioner	perceive
percentage	perception	perfect	performance
period	perish	permanent	permissible
permission	persevere	personal	personnel
persuade	pessimistic	petition	petrol
pharmacy	phase	phrase	physical
physique	picture	piece	pivot
placement	plaque	plastic	platform
plead	plenty	plight	plunge
poisonous	policing	policy	political
population	portable	portfolio	portion
position	positive	possession	possibility
postpone	posture	potential	practice
practising	practitioner	praise	precaution
precious	precise	predecessor	prediction
predominantly	preference	preferred	prejudice
preliminary	premature	premium	preparation
prescription	presence	presentation	preserve
pretence	preview	primary	priority
prison	private	privilege	probably
procedure	process	produce	professional
progression	prominent	promise	property
proprietor	prosecution	prospect	protection
protest	proved	provide	provoke
psychological	psychologist	publicity	publish
pulse	puncture	punishment	purchase
purpose	pursue	pursuit	quaint
qualification	qualify	quality	quantify
quantity	quarrelsome	quarter	quash
quell	questionable	queue	quickly
quiet	quite	quotation	racing
radiant	radical	radio	railing
random	range	rapid	rational
rationale	reaching	reactive	reading

realisation
recalled
recession
recommendation
recreation
recurrence
reference
refreshment
rehabilitation
related
relinquish
remote
repercussion
representation
residential
responsibility
restriction
retrenchment
rival
ruling
salvage
savoury
schedule
scratched
section
seizure
sentence
service
severe
signal
simultaneous
smear
solicitor
specialize
speculate
standard
stationery
subject
substance
suggest
supplement
surrendered
suspicion
technical
tangled
system
tentative
terminal

reality
recede
recipient
reconciliation
recruit
reduction
reflecting
refrigerator
reinforce
relationship
remaining
renowned
repetition
reprisal
resigned
responsible
resuscitate
reunited
robberies
sacrifice
sample
scald
scheme
search
security
selection
separate
session
shrewd
signature
situation
sociable
solution
specific
squander
staple
statistics
submerged
substitute
superintendent
suppose
survey
swallow
telephone
technological
target
temporary
territory

reasonable
receive
reckless
reconstruct
rectify
redundancy
reflex
refusal
rejection
release
remember
repair
replica
research
resources
restaurant
retention
review
rogue
safety
satellite
scandal
scholar
secondary
segment
sensible
sequence
settlement
shriek
significant
sizeable
society
sophisticated
specifically
square
static
statue
subsequent
succeed
superior
suppressed
susceptible
sympathy
telephonist
temperament
technology
terminated
tertiary

reassurance
reception
recognised
recovery
recuperate
redundant
reformed
registration
relapse
relief
remittance
repeated
reported
reservation
respectable
restitution
retirement
reward
rough
salary
savage
scarce
scientist
secretaries
seized
sensitive
sergeant
several
sign
silence
skilful
solemn
souvenir
specimen
stable
stationary
strength
subscription
sufficient
superstition
surge
suspend
tactic
syringe
tenant
temperature
termination
terrible

thirsty	thorough	theory	tissue
tobacco	thought	tongue	towards
tomorrow	traffic	tragedy	tradition
transfer	transparent	travelling	transport
triumph	trauma	truthful	turnover
trustworthy	ultimately	unaware	typical
unbelievable	unconscious	unbearable	undertaken
underrate	underground	uniform	union
unforeseen	unnecessary	unreliable	university
vacant	vacation	utilise	valuable
vandalism	vague	vehicle	venture
variation	version	vertical	verge
violence	visible	vigour	vocal
volume	vital	wager	warehouse
volunteer	wastage	waterproof	warrant
western	whereabouts	weapon	wilful
windcheater	whisper	withdrawal	worthy
window	wrong	wrongdoing	writing

Corrections
GCT Level 2

The General Competency Test: Level 2 (GCT2) measures an individual's general cognitive ability. There are 90 multiple-choice questions. The categories of the exam include:

- Vocabulary
- Number and Letter Series
- Analytical Reasoning
- Figural Relations
- Numerical Problems

The test takes 2 1/4 hours to write and the minimum pass mark is 51/90. If you are unsuccessful you must wait 180 days before you can rewrite the test.

Only paper, pencils and erasers are allowed - no books, dictionaries, notes, writing paper, calculators, calculator watches or other aids are permitted in the room.

Detach the answer key to take the test.

A B C D
1) ○○○○ ____
2) ○○○○ ____
3) ○○○○ ____
4) ○○○○ ____
5) ○○○○ ____
6) ○○○○ ____
7) ○○○○ ____
8) ○○○○ ____
9) ○○○○ ____
10) ○○○○ ____

A B C D E F G H
11) ○○○○ ○○○○ ____
12) ○○○○ ○○○○ ____
13) ○○○○ ○○○○ ____
14) ○○○○ ○○○○ ____
15) ○○○○ ○○○○ ____
16) ○○○○ ○○○○ ____
17) ○○○○ ○○○○ ____
18) ○○○○ ○○○○ ____
19) ○○○○ ○○○○ ____
20) ○○○○ ○○○○ ____

A B C D
21) ○○○○ ____
22) ○○○○ ____
23) ○○○○ ____
24) ○○○○ ____
25) ○○○○ ____
26) ○○○○ ____
27) ○○○○ ____
28) ○○○○ ____
29) ○○○○ ____
30) ○○○○ ____

A B C D
31) ○○○○ ____
32) ○○○○ ____
33) ○○○○ ____
34) ○○○○ ____
35) ○○○○ ____
36) ○○○○ ____
37) ○○○○ ____
38) ○○○○ ____
39) ○○○○ ____
40) ○○○○ ____

A B C D
41) ○○○○ ____
42) ○○○○ ____
43) ○○○○ ____
44) ○○○○ ____
45) ○○○○ ____
46) ○○○○ ____
47) ○○○○ ____
48) ○○○○ ____
49) ○○○○ ____
50) ○○○○ ____

A B C D
51) ○○○○ ____
52) ○○○○ ____
53) ○○○○ ____
54) ○○○○ ____
55) ○○○○ ____
56) ○○○○ ____
57) ○○○○ ____
58) ○○○○ ____
59) ○○○○ ____
60) ○○○○ ____

A B C D
61) ○○○○
62) ○○○○
63) ○○○○   E F G H
64) ○○○○ ○○○○
65) ○○○○ ○○○○
66) ○○○○ ____
67) ○○○○ ____
68) ○○○○ ____
69) ○○○○ ____
70) ○○○○ ____

A B C D
____ 71) ○○○○
____ 72) ○○○○
____ 73) ○○○○
____ 74) ○○○○
____ 75) ○○○○
76) ○○○○ ____
77) ○○○○ ____
78) ○○○○ ____
79) ○○○○ ____
80) ○○○○ ____

A B C D
81) ○○○○ ____
82) ○○○○ ____
83) ○○○○ ____
84) ○○○○ ____
85) ○○○○ ____
86) ○○○○ ____
87) ○○○○ ____
88) ○○○○ ____
89) ○○○○ ____
90) ○○○○ ____

Corrections Information

Every year approximately 2,000 people apply for a career with Corrections Canada. It is a very competitive process involving 6 components before you begin your career. Below is a brief description of the process. It is important to review the teaching material under the "Preparation" tab to ensure you are prepared for handing in your resume, performing your interviews and writing your exams.

Resume / Cover Letter

You will be required to submit a resume and cover letter explaining why you wish to have a career with Corrections Canada, how you are qualified, and why you should be selected. Recruiters with this organization seek as much information as possible. The information should be organized and relevant. Do not be afraid to submit a resume that is 2-3 pages in length. Read further information in the "Resume" teaching material.

Interview

Interviews with Corrections Canada are behavioural and values based. It is important to research and have knowledge of Corrections Canada, but you are not required to have knowledge of corrections procedures. Review additional material in our "Interview" teaching section.

Telephone Check

Corrections Canada will perform a telephone check of family members, friends, employers and references.

Medical / Background Check

A thorough background and medical check is performed including criminal and credit checks.

College Training

If successful, you will be invited to attend a 13-week training program involving eleven weeks of college and two weeks of institutional training. After successfully completing this program, you will be hired with Corrections Canada.

Question 1

The neighbourhood children are waiting for the bus. They are in kindergarten, grade 2, 3, 6, 7 and 9. Lisa is in a lower grade than Bonnie, but in a higher grade than Jimmy. Michael is in the lowest grade. Robert is in a grade lower than Jimmy. Bonnie is two grades lower than Rachael. Robert is older than Michael but younger than Jimmy. Rachael is oldest of all. Jimmy is three grades higher than Michael. What grade is Bonnie in?

a) 7th

b) 6th

c) 3rd

d) 9th

Question 2

The horse race is underway. The solid brown horse is ahead of the solid black horse, who is ahead of the white horse with black spots. The black horse with brown spots is trailing the white horse with brown spots. Which horse is in second place?

a) White with brown spots.

b) Solid brown.

c) Black with brown spots.

d) Solid black.

Question 3

Three girls on the gymnastics team recently completed a competition. Their events were beam, bars and floor. Amber placed second in beam, ahead of Elaine. Sarah was last on the bars, immediately behind Elaine. The team member who placed 2nd and 3rd in the other two events placed 1st in floor. What place did Sarah get on the beam?

a) 3rd

b) 2nd

c) 1st

d) 4th

Question 4

There are more employees working at noon than overnight. There are fewer employees working in the morning than in the evening. Morning and evening times require more employees than noon and overnight. Which shift uses the most employees?

a) Morning.

b) Evening.

c) Noon.

d) Overnight.

Question 5

Four women are talking about their favourite flower. They agree on Indian paintbrush, bluebonnet, daisy and rose. Each chooses a different favourite. Roberta likes the flower whose colour starts with the letter of her first name. Nancy's favourite colour is blue and so is her flower. Veronica does not like the Indian paintbrush. What is Tina's favourite flower?

a) Daisy.

b) Rose.

c) Indian paintbrush.

d) Bluebonnet.

Question 6

Students trying out for the swim team are tested to see how far they can swim. Gina has an asthma attack while in the water and has to stop swimming. Tina swims 10 metres less than Nina and 45 metres less than Christa. Who was able to swim the farthest?

a) Christa.   b) Tina.
c) Gina.   d) Nina.

Question 7

The men in an office decided to measure how much water they were drinking in a day. Ryan was drinking more than Tom. Jim was drinking less than Tom and Bob was drinking less than Jim. Who was drinking the second least amount of water each day?

a) Ryan.   b) Jim.
c) Bob.   d) Tom.

Question 8

The women in an office compared the different lengths of their hair. Britney has longer hair than Veronica, but shorter hair than Courtney. Lisa and Veronica have the same length of hair. Suzanne has longer hair than Julie. Julie has the same length of hair as Britney. Who in the office has medium-length hair?

a) Courtney and Lisa.   b) Julie and Lisa.
c) Veronica and Suzanne.   d) Britney and Julie.

Question 9

Some friends go to adopt a cat at the local pet store. There is an orange tabby, a white, long haired Persian, a tan Siamese with blue eyes and a calico mix. Julie does not like the colour white and is allergic to long fur. Charlie only likes long-haired cats and does not like cats with blue eyes. Leslie only likes blue-eyed cats and Danny does not mind a mixed cat. Julie's favourite color is orange. What cat does Charlie pick?

a) White Persian.   b) Tan Siamese.
c) Orange tabby.   d) Calico mix.

Question 10

The rehabilitation clinic sees more knee than neck problems. They see more shoulder problems than back problems. They see fewer shoulder problems than neck problems, but more knee than neck problems. What is the problem most often seen at the rehabilitation clinic?

a) Shoulder.   b) Neck.
c) Knee.   d) Back.

Question 11

Which is the missing image in the following patterns?

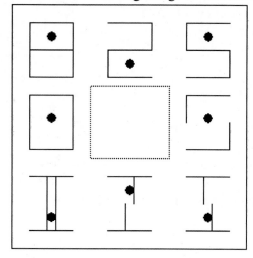

a)

b)

c)

d)

e)

f)

g)

h)

Question 12

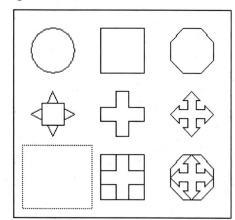

a)

b)

c)

d)

e)

f)

g)

h)

Question 13

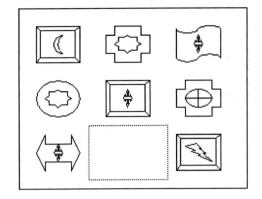

a)
b)
c)
d)

e)
f)
g)
h)

Question 14

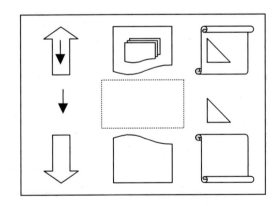

a)
b)
c)
d)

e)
f)
g)
h)

Question 15

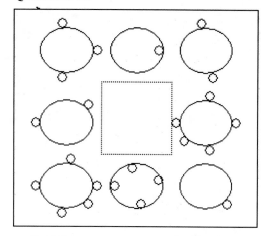

a)

b)

c)

d)

e)

f)

g)

h)

Question 16

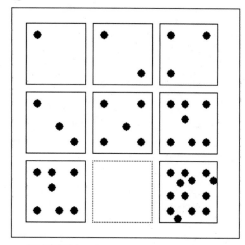

a)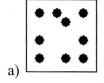

b)

c)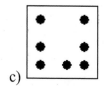

d)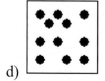

e)

f)

g)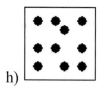

h)

Question 17

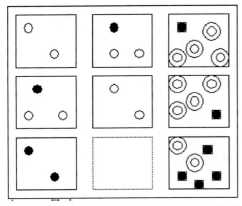

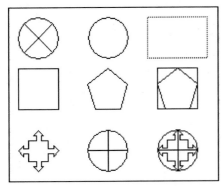 a)

 b)

 c)

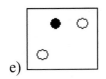 d)

 e)

 f)

 g)

 h)

Question 18

a)

 b)

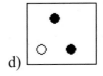 c)

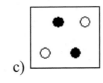 d)

 e)

 f)

 g)

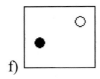 h)

Question 19

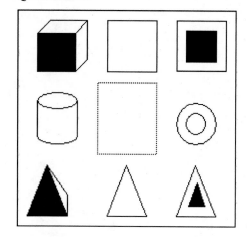

 a)   b)   c) ⬤   d)

 e)   f)   g) ⊕   h)

Question 20

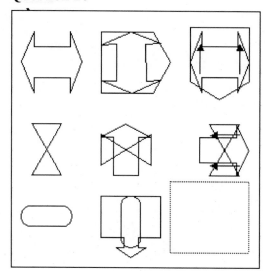

 a)   b)   c)   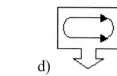 d)

e)   f)   g)   h)

Question 21

75 people came to the single's dance. If there were five more women than men, how many men were there?

a) 25

b) 30

c) 35

d) none of these

Question 22

Paulina is painting a picture on a canvas measuring 2 m by 3 m. She has painted 35% of the area. How much area is left to be painted?

a) 2.7 meters squared

b) 3.5 meters squared

c) 3.9 meters squared

d) 4.3 meters squared

Question 23

Natasha Kaya works 8 hours a day, 38 hours a week. She earns $6 an hour. How much will she earn in 3 weeks?

a) $226

b) $228

c) $660

d) $684

Question 24

A car stereo was stolen from a car outside of the pawn shop. It was originally purchased for $600. Street value is only 15% of the original purchase price. How much can the criminal resell the stereo for?

a) $15

b) $65

c) $70

d) $90

Question 25

140 pounds of drugs are confiscated during an arrest. There is marijuana, cocaine and crystal meth. If 20% of the drugs are cocaine and the remainder was made up of equal parts of marijuana and crystal meth, how many pounds of marijuana were confiscated?

a) 42 pounds

b) 50 pounds

c) 56 pounds

d) 62 pounds

Question 26

In phys. Ed class, Stephen Chan completed the 4 km run in 24 minutes. What is this speed in kilometres per hour?

a) 10

b) 11

c) 12

d) 13

Question 27

Solve for "x": $(7 - x) / 4 = x - 10$

a) 11.3

b) 9.4

c) 7.4

d) 5.3

Question 28
A sink holds 12 L of water. Water drains from it at a rate of 44 L a minute. How long would it take to empty the sink?

a) 1.2 minutes

b) 16 seconds

c) 12 seconds

d) 20 seconds

Question 29
Water flows through a pipe at 20,000 cm cubed per second. How many minutes does it take to fill a rectangular tank 3m x 4m x 5m?

a) 20 minutes

b) 35 minutes

c) 50 minutes

d) none of these

Question 30
There are 240 people at a picnic. People have a choice of cola or lemonade. For every two people that had a cola, one had a lemonade. How many people had cola?

a) 100

b) 160

c) 190

d) none of these

Question 31
If, when driving, you see a ball bounce into the road you should look for a _____ to come next.

a) bat

b) car

c) child

d) bicycle

Question 32
The young prince was so _____ , he laid his coat over a puddle for the princess to step over.

a) gallant

b) inhibited

c) passive

d) timid

Question 33
In the Middle Ages _____ were used to throw large stones over fortified walls.

a) pistols

b) catapults

c) shotguns

d) slingshots

Question 34
A country which does not take sides during a war or international crises is considered to be _____.

a) neutral

b) aggressive

c) threatening

d) chicken

Question 35

When an aquatic rescue is being made, Coast Guard officers need to avoid placing too much _____ on the rescue lines. This can cause the lines to snap.

a) laxity

b) strain

c) water

d) lubricant

Identify the synonym for the following words.

Question 36
Prototype

a) Archetype

b) Typewriter Ribbon

c) Standard

d) Oblique

Question 37
Arbitration

a) Severance

b) Mediation

c) Aggression

d) Channel

Question 38
Council

a) Advice

b) Judgment

c) Ruling Body

d) Encourage

Question 39
Revere

a) Turn Around

b) Despise

c) Respect

d) Coat Lapel

Question 40
Route

a) Intercourse

b) Direction

c) Challenge

d) Encourage

Question 41

Identify which number should replace the asterisk in the following questions.

	135	486
36	45	162
*	15	27

a) 6

b) 8

c) 10

d) None of the above.

Question 42

	203	207
195	197	199
189	191	*

a) 196

b) 193

c) 197

d) None of the above.

Question 43

12	48	*
6		96
3	12	48

a) 154

b) 176

c) 192

d) None of the above.

Question 44

4	12	72
2	6	*
1		18

a) 30

b) 36

c) 22

d) None of the above.

Question 45

103	354	*
225	476	727
	351	602

a) 601

b) 724

c) 607

d) None of the above.

Question 46

What are the missing numbers in the following patterns?
?, 16, 32, 64, 128, 256, ?...

a) 10, 524

b) 8, 512

c) 6, 412

d) None of the above.

Question 47

-14, ?, ?, 7, 14, 21...

a) -7, -1

b) -6, -1

c) -7, 0

d) None of the above.

Question 48

100, 97, 91, 82, 70, ?...

a) 61   b) 65

c) 67   d) None of the above.

Question 49

2, 8, 26, 80, ?...

a) 240   b) 232

c) 252   d) None of the above.

Question 50

?, 15, 27, 51, ?, 195...

a) 9, 93   b) 7, 97

c) 9, 99   d) None of the above.

Question 51

You are expecting an important shipment of auto parts. You placed the order three weeks ago, but the suppliers advised it would be running late. Four days ago you were advised that the parts were arriving in six days, and would immediately be shipped to you. You typically expect shipping to take two days. When should you expect the delivery?

a) 4 days   b) 2 weeks

c) 8 days   d) 10 days

Question 52

The ladies in the office wear different styles of pants and skirts. There are fewer long skirts than short skirts. There are fewer shorts than long skirts. There are more shorts than pants. Which type of clothing is the least prevalent in the office?

a) Short skirts.   b) Pants.

c) Long skirts.   d) Shorts.

Question 53

Four teams are playing in a tournament. Half way through the day, Team 4 is ahead of Team 1, but behind Team 2. Team 3 is ahead of Team 2 at this point in the day. Which team is in the same place as their team number?

a) Team 1.   b) Team 2.

c) Team 3.   d) Team 4.

Question 54

The family has decided to paint four rooms in the house: the kitchen, the dining room, the master bedroom and the guest bathroom. The kitchen is larger than the guest bathroom, but smaller than the dining room. The master bedroom is not smaller than any of the rooms. Which room will take the least amount of paint?

a) Dining room.   b) Master bedroom.

c) Kitchen.   d) Guest bathroom.

Question 55

The customer service department determines bonuses paid based on the number of calls an employee completes each day. Kristina handles twice as many calls as Frank. Frank handles more calls than Natalie. Angela handles as many as Natalie and Frank combined. Which operator handles the most calls?

a) Frank.   b) Angela.

c) Natalie.   d) Kristina.

Question 56

What are the next items in the patterns below?

a)   b)

c)   d)

Question 57

Apple, cat, enigma, giraffe...

a) Ostrich, umbrella, guinea   b) Insane, kitten, monkey

c) Stop, under, yak   d) Cantaloupe, quill, wombat

Question 58

Apple, car, bat, dingo, cover, engine…

a) Oat, nickel, simple, rhinoceros

b) Elephant, jungle, tipped, car

c) Dent, fox, elbow, goose

d) Quail, walrus, x-ray, zebra

Question 59

a)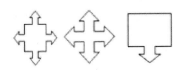

b)

c)

d)

Question 60

a)

b)

c)

d)

Question 61

a)

b)

c)

d)

Question 62

a)

b)

c)

d)

Question 63

AB YZ CD WX EF ...

a) OP GH KL ST

b) UV JK NO AB

c) UV GH OP IJ

d) QR KL MN ST

Question 64

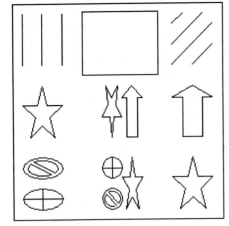

 a)
 b)
c)
d)

 e)
 f)
 g)
 h)

Question 65

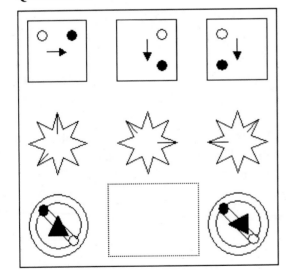

 a)
 b)
c)
 d)

 e)
 f)
g)
 h)
 h)
 h)

Question 66

Rita is able to read 30 pages an hour. For an assignment she has two books to read. The first book has 1,350 pages and the second book has 2,010 pages. How many hours will it take Rita to finish both books?

a) 75
b) 110
c) 112
d) 121

Question 67

A car can accelerate at 5 kph per second. How much time will it take the car to reach 75 kph?

a) 15 seconds
b) 22 seconds
c) 25 seconds
d) 27 seconds

Question 68

John travels 75 KM to work each way. If he averages 120 kph, how many minutes does he spend driving to and from work each day?

a) 1.25
b) 75
c) 50
d) 60

Question 69

An officer's quota for speeding tickets each month is 0.5% of the average traffic flow on Highway 401. Each month the average flow is 13 million cars. If the officer has issued 50,000 tickets at mid-month, how many more tickets are needed to reach the quota?

a) 25,000
b) 15,000
c) 20,000
d) 30,000

Question 70

Students want to convert a spare room into a lab. The room space is 10' x 10'. A lab needs to have 120 square feet minimum for ventilation. How many more square feet are needed for this lab to be a "safe" environment to enter?

a) 30
b) 50
c) 40
d) 20

Question 71

A truck trailer is filled with explosives. The dimensions of the trailer are 25' x 10' x 15'. The explosives are in crates measuring 5' x 5' x 5'. How many crates of explosives can fit in the truck?

a) 27
b) 30
c) 42
d) 51

Question 72

There are 10 Caucasian, 14 African American and 12 Hispanic people in the office. If there are an equal number of men and women of each race, how many African American women are in the office?

a) 6   b) 7

c) 5   d) 18

Question 73

The average amount of snowfall in Maine increases by 6% each year. If the snowfall amount was 23 inches in 2001, what will the snowfall amount be in 2006?

a) 25.8 inches   b) 27.4 inches

c) 29.0 inches   d) 30.8 inches

Question 74

A park is planned and will be 3 city blocks by 3 city blocks in size. Each city block is 20 metres in length. What is the total area covered by the new park?

a) 1600 square metres   b) 2400 square metres

c) 3600 square metres   d) 4200 square metres

Question 75

A new, entry-level employee makes $23,000 per year. If the salary level increases by 2% after every 3 years of service, what will her salary be after 8 years of work?

a) $23,460   b) $23,929

c) $24,408   d) $24,168

Identify the synonym for the following words.

Question 76

Irksome

a) Annoying   b) Irrational

c) Sour   d) Diseased

Question 77

Arraign

a) Sue   b) Confess

c) Exonerate   d) Prosecute

Question 78

Arduous

a) Clever   b) Emotional

c) Difficult   d) Thoughtful

Question 79

Perjury

a) Lying Under Oath	b) Testimony
c) Evidence	d) Selecting a Jury

Question 80

Pedestrians

a) Motorists	b) Toys
c) Athletes	d) Citizens on Foot

Question 81

What number should replace the asterisk in the following questions?

	32	18
154	23	9
145	14	*

a) 1	b) 3
c) 6	d) None of the above.

Question 82

21	63	*
3	9	27
	48	144

a) 81	b) 189
c) 154	d) None of the above.

Question 83

4	100	500
12	300	1500
	900	*

a) 3000	b) 3500
c) 4500	d) None of the above.

Question 84

3	12	48
	24	96
12	48	*

a) 192	b) 208
c) 480	d) None of the above.

Question 85

	3	18
2	6	*
4	12	72

a) 32

b) 36

c) 42

d) None of the above.

Question 86

What are the missing numbers in the following patterns?

1, ?, ?, 27, 81, 243, 729...

a) 3, 12

b) 4, 9

c) 3, 9

d) None of the above.

Question 87

2, ?, 4, 9, 6, 11, 8...

a) 6

b) 7

c) 8

d) None of the above.

Question 88

50, 0, 0, -40, -40, -70, -70, -90, -90, ?, ?...

a) -95, -100

b) -95, -95

c) -100, -100

d) None of the above.

Question 89

6, 16, 36, 76, 156, ?...

a) 316

b) 286

c) 356

d) None of the above.

Question 90

2, 4, ?, 256...

a) 12

b) 16

c) 20

d) None of the above.

1) A	26) A	51) A	76) A
2) D	27) B	52) B	77) D
3) C	28) B	53) B	78) C
4) B	29) C	54) D	79) A
5) C	30) B	55) D	80) D
6) A	31) C	56) C	81) D
7) B	32) A	57) B	82) B
8) D	33) B	58) C	83) C
9) A	34) A	59) D	84) A
10) C	35) B	60) B	85) B
11) C	36) A	61) D	86) C
12) E	37) B	62) A	87) B
13) A	38) C	63) C	88) C
14) E	39) C	64) B	89) A
15) B	40) B	65) G	90) B
16) H	41) D	66) C	
17) C	42) B	67) A	
18) E	43) C	68) B	
19) C	44) B	69) B	
20) H	45) D	70) D	
21) C	46) B	71) B	
22) C	47) C	72) B	
23) D	48) D	73) D	
24) D	49) D	74) C	
25) C	50) C	75) B	

Question 1

The children from the lowest to highest grade are: Michael, Robert, Jimmy, Lisa, Bonnie and then Rachael.

Question 2

The order of the horses from first to last is: solid brown, solid black, white with brown spots and then black with brown spots.

Question 3

The places of the girls on the beam from first to last are: Sarah, Amber and then Elaine.

Question 4

The order of employees, working from most to least, is: evening, morning, noon and then overnight.

Question 5

The women and their best-liked flower are as follows: Tina-Indian Paintbrush, Roberta-Rose, Veronica-daisy, Nancy-bluebonnets.

Question 6

The order that the girls could swim, from farthest to least, is: Christa, Nina, Tina, and then Gina.

Question 7

The order of water consumption from highest to lowest is: Ryan, Tom, Jim and then Bob.

Question 8

The girls with short hair are Veronica and Lisa, with medium hair are Britney and Julie, and with long hair are Courtney and Suzanne.

Question 9

Julie picks the orange tabby, Charlie picks the white Persian, Leslie picks the tan Siamese, and Danny picks the calico mix.

Question 10

The order of problems seen, from most to least, is: knee, neck, shoulder and then back.

Question 11

From left to right, the top left and bottom right line are lost. Then the top right and bottom left line are lost. Dots alternate from top to bottom to top on the top line, straight across on the middle line and bottom top bottom on the bottom line.

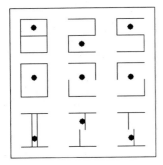

Question 12

An object from first row is superimposed on an object from the second row to create an object in the third row.

Question 13

Outside shapes remain consistent as you travel diagonally from top left to bottom right. Inside shapes remain consistent as you travel diagonally from top right to bottom left.

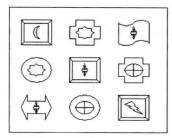

Question 14

The row consists of superimposing the middle row on the mirror image of the bottom row.

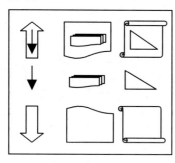

Question 15

Circles on outside represent positive integers; circles on the inside represent negative integers.

Row one is added to row two resulting in row three. (3 − 1 = 2, 2 + 3 = 5, 5 − 4 = 1)

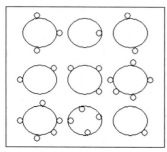

Question 16

The number of dots in the first row increases by one from left to right. The number of dots in the second row increases by two from left to right and by three in the third row.

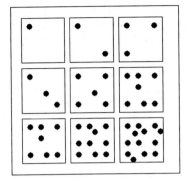

Question 17

To determine the third column, the shapes in the first column are added to the shapes in the second column. The black circles are covered by a black square in the third column, and the white circles are surrounded by another circle.

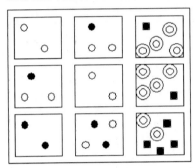

Question 18

The shapes from column one are superimposed on the shapes from column two which results in column three.

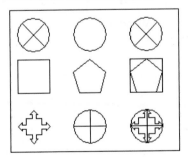

Question 19

A three-dimensional object in column one is followed by a two-dimensional object in column two, which is followed by a double image. Solid black shapes cross diagonally.

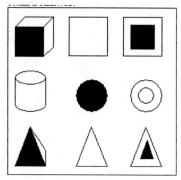

Question 20

The object in column one rotates 90 degrees clockwise in column two and a further 90 degrees in column three. The object that first appears in column two rotates 90 degrees clockwise in column three. The arrows that first appear in column three point in the opposite direction of the object that first appears in column two.

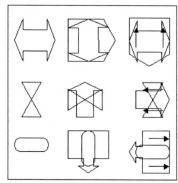

Question 21

To solve this problem, set up an algebraic equation. "Y" will represent the number of men and the number of women will equal y + 5. When you add the women to the men, the total is 75.

$$y + y + 5 = 75$$
$$2y + 5 = 75 \qquad \text{Therefore, there are 35 men at the dance.}$$
$$2y = 70$$
$$y = 35$$

Question 22

First, determine the total area of the canvas. 2m x 3m = 6 square metres.
Second, determine how much has been painted. 6 x 35% = 2.1 metres.
Finally, determine how much is left to be painted 6 – 2.1 = 3.9 square metres.

Question 23

Determine how much money is made in one week (38 x $6 = $228), and then multiply that total by the number of weeks ($228 x 3 = $684).

Question 24
600 x 15% = 90

Question 25
140 x 0.2 = 28 lbs. of cocaine. 140–28 = 112 lbs. remaining. 112/2 = 56 lbs. of marijuana.

Question 26
An algebraic equation will be required for this question.

$\dfrac{4 \text{ km}}{y \text{ km}} = \dfrac{24 \text{ minutes}}{60 \text{ minutes}}$ Multiply both sides by "y". $4 = \dfrac{24\,y}{60}$

Multiply both sides by 60. $240 = 24\,y$ then divide both sides by 24. $10 = y$

Stephen Chan was running at 10 km per hour.

Question 27
An algebraic equation will be required for this question.

$\dfrac{(7 - x)}{4} = x - 10$ Multiply both sides by 4. $7 - x = 4x - 40$

Add 40 to each side. $47 - x = 4x$ Add y to both sides. $47 = 5x$

Finally divide both sides by 5. $47/5 = x = 9.4$.

Question 28
First, determine how many litres are drained each second. 44 litres / 60 seconds = 0.73. Therefore, 0.73 litres are drained from the sink each second.

Second, divide 0.73 litres into the 12 litre capacity of the sink. 0.73 / 12 = 16.4 seconds.

Question 29
First, calculate the total volume of the tank. 300 x 400 x 500 = 60,000,000 cubic cm. Second, determine the number of seconds that it will take to fill the tank. Divide the volume by the rate the water is flowing.
     6,000,000 / 20,000 = 3,000 minutes to fill the tank.
Finally, convert 3,000 seconds to minutes. 3,000 / 60 = 50 minutes to fill the tank.

Question 30
First, set up an algebraic equation where "y" represents the number of people who had a cola. ½ y would be the number of people who had lemonade.
     y + ½ y = 240 or 1.5 y = 240
To isolate "y" divide both sides by 1.5.
     y = 240/1.5 = 160 people were drinking cola.

Question 31

"Child" would be the most logical answer, as they would be most likely to chase the ball.

Question 32

"Gallant" is the correct answer, meaning courteous or chivalrous.

Question 33

A "catapult" is an older weapon that flung large rocks like missiles.

Question 34

"Neutral" means refusing to take sides.

Question 35

"Strain" is the most likely cause of a rope snapping.

Refer to the Answer Key for answers to questions 36-40

Question 41

Multiplying

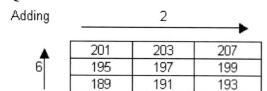

3

108	135	486
36	45	162
12	15	27

Question 42

Adding   2

6

201	203	207
195	197	199
189	191	193

Question 43

Multiplying   4

2

12	48	192
6	24	96
3	12	48

Question 44

Multiplying   3   6

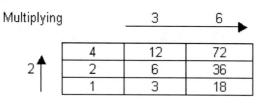

2

4	12	72
2	6	36
1	3	18

Question 45

Adding   251 →

103	354	605
225	476	727
100	351	602

Question 46

The numbers are increasing by multiples of 2. (8, 16, 32, 64, 128, 256, 512...).

Question 47

The numbers are being added by 7. (-7. 0, 7, 14, 21, 28...).

Question 48

The numbers are declining by multiples of 3 in the following pattern: -3, -6, -9, -12 etc. (100, 97, 91, 82, 70, 55, ...)

Question 49

The numbers are being multiplied by 3 and then added by 2 (2, 8, 26, 80, 242...).

Question 50

The numbers are being multiplied by 2 and subtracted by 3 (9, 15, 27, 51, 99, 195...).

Question 51

If you spoke with the supplier four days ago and they advised the parts would be shipped in 6 days that means the parts will be shipped in 2 days. Add another 2 days for shipping and the answer is 4 days.

Question 52

The order of items, from most to least worn, is: short skirts, long skirts, shorts and then pants.

Question 53

The teams are in the following places, from first to last: Team 3, Team 2, Team 4, and then Team 1.

Question 54

The amount of paint needed by room, from most to least is: bedroom, dining room, kitchen, and then bathroom.

Question 55

Natalie handles fewer calls than Frank, so their combined total would not be as high as doubling Frank's production. Kristina, therefore, takes the most calls.

Question 56

If you go to school, ask questions, take the test and get A's, you will graduate next.

Question 57

The first letter of each word skips every second letter of the alphabet (A, C, E, G...)

Question 58

The first letter of each word skips a letter, then goes back one, then skips one, etc.

Question 59

Round brackets convert to curved brackets vertically. The same process is repeated horizontally.

Question 60

The block is in the centre of arrows, then the block is gone. The block is at the top of the arrow, then the block is gone.

Question 61

The pattern goes from small dots to wavy lines and repeats.

Question 62

The first star has 8 points. These points increase by 8 so that the final star has 32 points.

Question 63

First two letters of the alphabet are followed by the last two. The next letters are the third and fourth letters of the alphabet followed by the third and fourth last letters of the alphabet. The next would be fifth and sixth letters of the alphabet, followed by the fifth and sixth last letters of the alphabet and so on...

Question 64

The middle column is a compressed merger of the first and second columns. The image from the first column is also rotated 180 degrees.

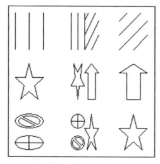

Question 65

The mages rotates 90 degrees between columns 1 and 2. Column 3 is a mirror image of column 2.

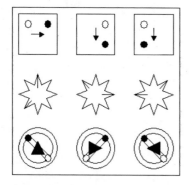

Question 66

First, calculate the total number of pages Rita must read [1,350 + 2,010 = 3,360]. Then, divide the total number pages by her reading speed [3,360/30 = 112 minutes].

Question 67

75/5=15   It will take 15 seconds to accelerate to 75 kph.

Question 68

Calculate John's total return trip driving distance [75 + 75 = 150KM]. Then divide total distance by his average driving speed [150/120=1.25hr]. Then convert 1.25 hours to minutes by multiplying by 60, to arrive at 75 minutes.

Question 69

13,000,000 x 0.005=65,000

65,000 - 50,000 = 15,000 tickets

Question 70

10 x 10 = 100 square feet

120 – 100 = 20 square feet

Question 71

25 x 10 x 15 = 3750 cubic feet

5 x 5 x 5 = 125 cubic feet

3750 / 125 = 30 boxes

Question 72

14 / 2 = 7

Question 73

2002: 23 x 1.06 = 24.38   2003: 24.38 x 1.06 = 25.84   2004: 25.84 x 1.06 = 27.39

2005: 27.39 x 1.06 = 29.036   2006: 29.036 x 1.06 = 30.8

Question 74

The perimeter would be 60 metres by 60 metres (20 x 3 = 60). The area would be 60 x 60 = 3600 square metres.

Question 75

Eight years of employment would provide 2 pay increases.

23,000 x 1.02 = $23,460   23,460 x 1.02 = $23,939

Refer to the Answer Key for answers to questions 76-80
Question 81

Adding

9

163	32	18
154	23	9
145	14	0

Question 82

Multiplying

3

21	63	189
3	9	27
16	48	144

Question 83

Multiplying

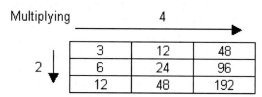

Question 84

Multiplying

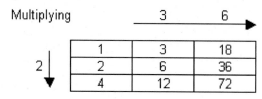

Question 85

Multiplying

	3	6
1	3	18
2	6	36
4	12	72

2 ↓

Question 86

The numbers are increasing by multiples of 3 (1, 3, 9, 27, 81, 243, 729...)

Question 87

The numbers grow by 5 then decrease by 3 (2, 7, 4, 9, 6, 11, 8...).

Question 88

The pattern is subtracting a declining multiple of 10 (50 then 40 then 30 etc.), followed by subtracting 0. -50, -0, -40, -0, -30, -0, -20, -0, etc. (50, 0, 0, -40, -40, -70, -70, -90, -90, -100, -100...).

Question 89

The numbers are being added by 2 and then multiplied by 2 (6, 16, 36, 76, 156, 316,...).

Question 90

The numbers are being squared (2, 4, 16, 256, 65536...).

Answer Sheet BSOT – Book 2

Facial Recognition (4 pts each)

	A	B	C	D	
1)	○	○	○	○	_____
2)	○	○	○	○	_____
3)	○	○	○	○	_____
4)	○	○	○	○	_____
5)	○	○	○	○	_____

Total   / 20   _____

Similarity (4 pts each)

	A	B	C	D	
6)	○	○	○	○	_____
7)	○	○	○	○	_____
8)	○	○	○	○	_____
9)	○	○	○	○	_____
10)	○	○	○	○	_____
11)	○	○	○	○	_____
12)	○	○	○	○	_____
13)	○	○	○	○	_____
14)	○	○	○	○	_____
15)	○	○	○	○	_____

Total   / 40   _____

Identification (7 pts each)

	A	B	C	D	
16)	○	○	○	○	_____
17)	○	○	○	○	_____
18)	○	○	○	○	_____
19)	○	○	○	○	_____
20)	○	○	○	○	_____
21)	○	○	○	○	_____
22)	○	○	○	○	_____
23)	○	○	○	○	_____
24)	○	○	○	○	_____
25)	○	○	○	○	_____

Total   / 70   _____

Judgment (12 pts each)

	A	B	C	D	
26)	○	○	○	○	_____
27)	○	○	○	○	_____
28)	○	○	○	○	_____
29)	○	○	○	○	_____
30)	○	○	○	○	_____

Total   / 60   _____

Premise / Assumption (12 pts each)

	A	B	C	D	
31)	○	○	○	○	_____
32)	○	○	○	○	_____
33)	○	○	○	○	_____
34)	○	○	○	○	_____
35)	○	○	○	○	_____

Total   / 60   _____

Mapping (12 pts each)

	A	B	C	D	
36)	○	○	○	○	_____
37)	○	○	○	○	_____
38)	○	○	○	○	_____
39)	○	○	○	○	_____
40)	○	○	○	○	_____

Total   / 60

Total _____ / 310

Answer Sheet BSOT – Book 4

Memory of Suspects (8 pts each)

	A	B	C	D	
1)	○	○	○	○	_____
2)	○	○	○	○	_____
3)	○	○	○	○	_____
4)	○	○	○	○	_____
5)	○	○	○	○	_____
6)	○	○	○	○	_____
7)	○	○	○	○	_____
8)	○	○	○	○	_____
9)	○	○	○	○	_____
10)	○	○	○	○	_____

Total   / 80   _____

By-Law (6 pts each)

	A	B	C	D	E	
11)	○	○	○	○	○	_____
12)	○	○	○	○	○	_____
13)	○	○	○	○	○	_____
14)	○	○	○	○	○	_____
15)	○	○	○	○	○	_____
16)	○	○	○	○	○	_____
17)	○	○	○	○	○	_____
18)	○	○	○	○	○	_____
19)	○	○	○	○	○	_____
20)	○	○	○	○	○	_____
21)	○	○	○	○	○	_____
22)	○	○	○	○	○	_____
23)	○	○	○	○	○	_____
24)	○	○	○	○	○	_____
25)	○	○	○	○	○	_____

Total   / 90   _____

Total: _____ / 310

Rules (10 pts each)

	A	B	C	D	
26)	○	○	○	○	_____
27)	○	○	○	○	_____
28)	○	○	○	○	_____
29)	○	○	○	○	_____
30)	○	○	○	○	_____
31)	○	○	○	○	_____
32)	○	○	○	○	_____
33)	○	○	○	○	_____

Total   / 80   _____

Memory (5 pts each)

	A	B	C	D	
34)	○	○	○	○	_____
35)	○	○	○	○	_____
36)	○	○	○	○	_____
37)	○	○	○	○	_____
38)	○	○	○	○	_____
39)	○	○	○	○	_____
40)	○	○	○	○	_____
41)	○	○	○	○	_____
42)	○	○	○	○	_____
43)	○	○	○	○	_____
44)	○	○	○	○	_____
45)	○	○	○	○	_____

Total   / 60   _____

Answer Sheet BSOT – Book 5

Forms (3 pts each)

	A	B	C	D	E	
1)	○	○	○	○	○	_____
2)	○	○	○	○	○	_____
3)	○	○	○	○	○	_____
4)	○	○	○	○	○	_____
5)	○	○	○	○	○	_____
6)	○	○	○	○	○	_____
7)	○	○	○	○	○	_____
8)	○	○	○	○	○	_____
9)	○	○	○	○	○	_____
10)	○	○	○	○	○	_____

Total / 30   _____

Math (4 pts each)

	A	B	C	D	
11)	○	○	○	○	_____
12)	○	○	○	○	_____
13)	○	○	○	○	_____
14)	○	○	○	○	_____
15)	○	○	○	○	_____
16)	○	○	○	○	_____
17)	○	○	○	○	_____
18)	○	○	○	○	_____
19)	○	○	○	○	_____
20)	○	○	○	○	_____

Total / 40   _____

Spelling (2 pts each)

	A	B	C	D	
21)	○	○	○	○	_____
22)	○	○	○	○	_____
23)	○	○	○	○	_____
24)	○	○	○	○	_____
25)	○	○	○	○	_____
26)	○	○	○	○	_____
27)	○	○	○	○	_____

Total / 14   _____

Vocabulary (2 pts each)

	A	B	C	D	
28)	○	○	○	○	_____
29)	○	○	○	○	_____
30)	○	○	○	○	_____
31)	○	○	○	○	_____
32)	○	○	○	○	_____
33)	○	○	○	○	_____
34)	○	○	○	○	_____
35)	○	○	○	○	_____
36)	○	○	○	○	_____
37)	○	○	○	○	_____

Total / 20   _____

Grammar (3 pts each)

	A	B	C	D	
38)	○	○	○	○	_____
39)	○	○	○	○	_____
40)	○	○	○	○	_____
41)	○	○	○	○	_____
42)	○	○	○	○	_____
43)	○	○	○	○	_____

Total / 18   _____

Reading Comprehension (5 pts each)

	A	B	C	D	
44)	○	○	○	○	_____
45)	○	○	○	○	_____
46)	○	○	○	○	_____
47)	○	○	○	○	_____
48)	○	○	○	○	_____
49)	○	○	○	○	_____
50)	○	○	○	○	_____
51)	○	○	○	○	_____
52)	○	○	○	○	_____
53)	○	○	○	○	_____

Total / 50   _____

Forms (3 pts each)

	A	B	C	D	E	
54)	O	O	O	O	O	_____
55)	O	O	O	O	O	_____
56)	O	O	O	O	O	_____
57)	O	O	O	O	O	_____
58)	O	O	O	O	O	_____
59)	O	O	O	O	O	_____
60)	O	O	O	O	O	_____
61)	O	O	O	O	O	_____
62)	O	O	O	O	O	_____
63)	O	O	O	O	O	_____

Total / 30   _____

Math (4 pts each)

	A	B	C	D	
64)	O	O	O	O	_____
65)	O	O	O	O	_____
66)	O	O	O	O	_____
67)	O	O	O	O	_____
68)	O	O	O	O	_____

Total   / 20   _____

Spelling (2 pts each)

	A	B	C	D	
69)	O	O	O	O	_____
70)	O	O	O	O	_____
71)	O	O	O	O	_____
72)	O	O	O	O	_____
73)	O	O	O	O	_____
74)	O	O	O	O	_____
75)	O	O	O	O	_____

Total   / 14   _____

Total _____ / 284

Vocabulary (2 pts each)

	A	B	C	D	
76)	O	O	O	O	_____
77)	O	O	O	O	_____
78)	O	O	O	O	_____
79)	O	O	O	O	_____
80)	O	O	O	O	_____

Total   / 10   _____

Grammar (3 pts each)

	A	B	C	D	E	
81)	O	O	O	O		_____
82)	O	O	O	O		_____
83)	O	O	O	O		_____
84)	O	O	O	O		_____
85)	O	O	O	O	O	_____
86)	O	O	O	O	O	_____

Total   / 18   _____

Reading Comprehension (5 pts each)

	A	B	C	D	
87)	O	O	O	O	_____
88)	O	O	O	O	_____
89)	O	O	O	O	_____
90)	O	O	O	O	_____

Total   / 20   _____

Border Services Officer Test (BSOT)

The Border Services Officer Test is a lengthy examination process, which takes several hours to complete. The exam and the preparation material on this site are broken down in the following manner:

Book 1 – 20 minutes

A study guide containing pictures of suspects with descriptions, along with a list of rules and by-laws is provided that you have 20 minutes to study and memorize. You are not permitted to write any of this information down.

Book 2 – 60 minutes

5 Facial Recognition (4 points each)
10 Identification (7 points each)
3 Premise (12 points each)
5 Mapping (12 points each)

10 Similarity (4 points each)
5 Judgment (12 points each)
2 Assumption (12 points each)

Book 3 – 2 minutes

A study guide containing pictures that you will have 2 minutes to study and memorize. You are not permitted to write any of this information down.

Book 4 – 20 minutes

10 Memory of Suspects (8 points each)
8 Rules (10 points each)

15 By-Law (6 points each)
12 Memory of Pictures (5 points each)

Book 5 – 1 hour 15 minutes

20 Form (3 points each)
14 Spelling (2 points each)
12 Grammar (3 points each)

15 Math (3-4 points each)
15 Vocabulary (2 points each)
14 Reading Comp. (5 points each)

You must perform the books in order. Books 1 - 4 must be performed in one sitting as the information is related. You are permitted a half hour break before beginning Book 5. Paper, pencils and erasers are allowed - no books, dictionaries, notes, writing paper, calculators, calculator watches or other aids are to be taken into the room.

You have 5 minutes to memorize the information on the following two pages. You will be questioned about it at the beginning of Book 3. You are not allowed to write down any of the information.

Name: Brad Jeffersen
Gender: Male
Age: 26
Eye Colour: Blue
Identifying Features: Scar Upper Back
Crime Wanted For: Drinking and Driving

Name: Shane Domi
Gender: Male
Age: 30
Eye Colour: Green
Identifying Features: Birthmark Right Knee
Crime Wanted For: Theft

Make:
2002 Dodge Ram
Colour:
Red
License:
998 YRE
Crime:
Murder

Make:
2001 Buick Century
Colour:
Maroon
License:
453 NMS
Crime:
Hit and Run

Make:
1998 Honda Accord
Colour:
Black
License:
422 PIB
Crime:
Theft

Name: Jesse Kolovak
Gender: Male
Age: 33
Eye Colour: Blue
Identifying Features: Scar Left Shoulder
Crime Wanted For: Kidnapping

Name: Narish Jamal
Gender: Male
Age: 44
Eye Colour: Brown
Identifying Features: Missing left index finger
Crime Wanted For: Aggravated Assault

Make:
1998 Toyota Camry
Colour:
Grey
License:
308 FDR
Crime:
Kidnapping

Make:
1998 Toyota 4 Run
Colour:
Black
License:
306 KLM
Crime:
Assault

Make:
1994 Volks Golf
Colour:
Red
License:
581 GHD
Crime:
Sexual Assault

Kitchen Rules:

All drawers must remain closed at all times.
Towels must remain hanging to dry.
No food is to be left on the counter top.
Knives must be kept safe and secure at all times.
All food stored in the cupboards must be sealed.
Water must not be left running.
The stove must be kept off unless cooking.
Dishes must be kept off the counter top.
The sink must be emptied at all times.
The stovetop must be kept clear of all obstacles.
Pots must be stored in the upper cupboards.

By-Laws

Any person parking on the street must live in the home that the vehicle is parked in front of.
If the person does not live there, written consent must be gotten from the owner of the home.
It is never acceptable for a vehicle to be parked on the grass or over the curb.
If your vehicle is towed, contact the county clerk's office to arrange a pickup.
If your vehicle is parked in the driveway, it needs to be pulled to the front.
No more than 2 cars may be parked in the driveway.

Question 1

Which of the following people matches this suspect?

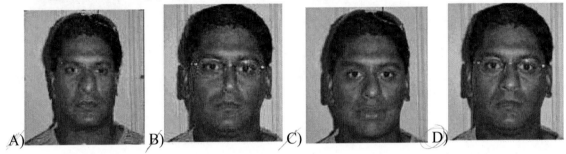

A)   B)   C)   D)

Question 2

Which of the following people matches this suspect?

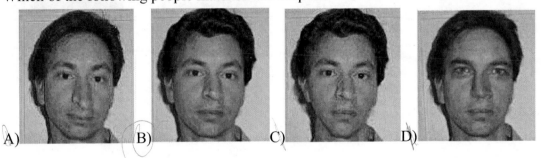

A)   B)   C)   D)

Question 3

Which of the following people matches this suspect?

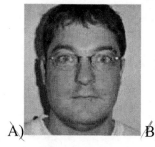

A)

B)

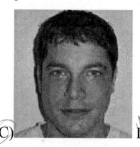

C)

D)

Question 4

Which of the following people matches this suspect?

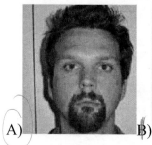

A)

B)

C)

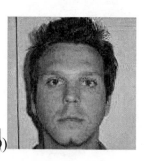

D)

Question 5

Which of the following people matches this suspect?

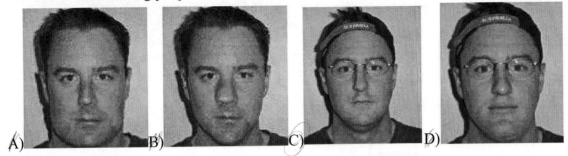

A)   B)   C)   D)

For the following questions, select the image that best matches the one on top.

Question 6

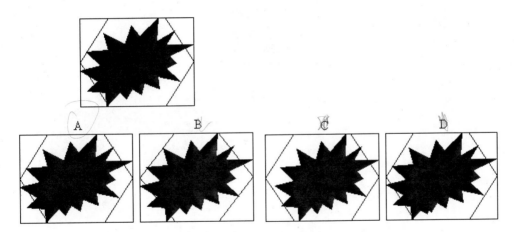

A   B   C   D

Question 7

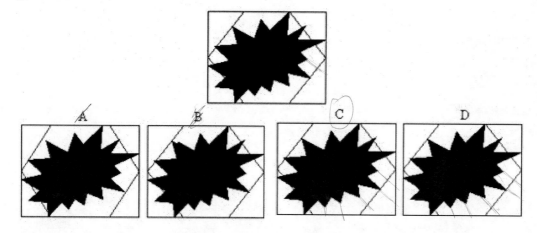

Question 8

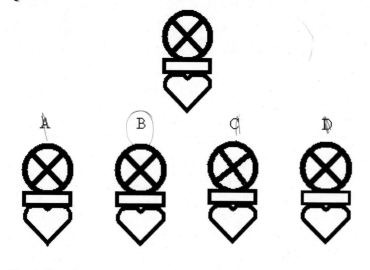

Question 9

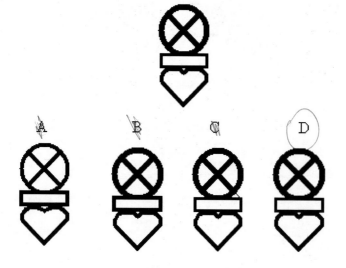

Question 10

Question 11

Question 12

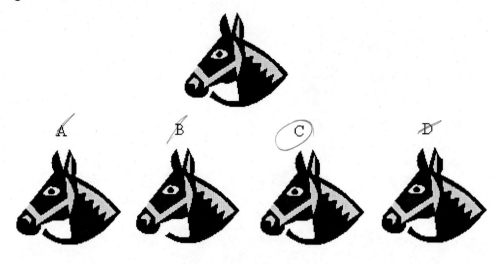

Question 13

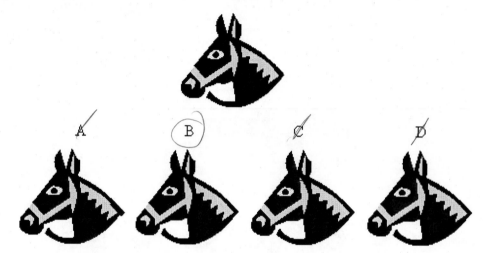

Question 14

Question 15

Which of the following images is the best match to the one on top?

The following questions are based on the pictures below.

Question 16

What is the person wearing the jeans by the tree carrying?

a) Briefcase

b) Coffee Cup

c) Black Knapsack

d) Water bottle

Question 17

What is the name of the coffee shop?

a) Baroli

b) Olibar

c) Barold

d) Labrodi

Question 18

In the photo with the escalator, how many levels can be seen in the mall?

a) 1

b) 2

c) 3

d) 4

Question 19

What object is left of the tree?

a) Information counter   b) Fire hydrant

c) Garbage can   d) Billboard

Question 20

How many people were going down the escalator?

a) 1   b) 2   c) 3   d) 4

Question 21

Which of the following statements is true about the outside picture?

a) The hydrant is gushing water.

b) There is an advertisement in the background displaying a car.

c) There is a man wearing shorts and white shoes in the picture with the fire hydrant.

d) There is a person carrying a black bag walking from right to left by the fire hydrant.

Question 22

Which of the following statements is true?

a) Baroli is located in the basement.

b) There are 3 people in line at Baroli.

c) There is a person in line at Baroli wearing a backpack.

d) None of the above.

Question 23

What is the advertisement on the escalator most likely for?

a) Coffee   b) Automobile

c) Education   d) Hair Products

Question 24

Which of the following statements are true based on the picture with the art show?

a) The pallet is on the forklift.   b) The department store appears closed.

c) There are three pallets visible.   d) None of the above.

Question 25

How many stepladders can be seen in the art show?

a) 1   b) 2

c) 3   d) 4

Question 26

You are working as a solo unit and you receive a call from a dispatcher to attend a noise complaint from Mrs. Smith for an unruly group of teenagers in the local park. A neighbour called in the complaint stating she believed that they were smoking drugs. You pull up to the park in your cruiser and view a group of 7 individuals in their late teens / early 20's sitting on at a picnic table approximately 50 meters away. What is the first action you should take?

a) Ask dispatcher if there is any available back up.

b) Approach the group on your own.

c) Walk around the park and see if there are any other groups.

d) Call the members of the group to come over to your vehicle.

Question 27

Dispatcher advises that there is back up available and will be there within 10 minutes. Which is the next action you should take?

a) Back up will take too long, approach the group on your own.

b) Give back up a couple minutes, but approach if they spot you and begin to leave.

c) Wait for back up before approaching.

d) Approach with a fellow citizen as support.

Question 28

You feel uneasy about the group as you are talking to them with your partner. None of the group members has done anything wrong in front of you. Which approach is justifiable?

a) Search the members of the group for weapons or drugs.

b) Tell the group members you want them to keep their hands where you can see them.

c) Split the group up so that you deal with one section of the group and your partner takes his section to a different area.

d) None of the above. You are not justified in doing any of the above.

Question 29

While on patrol Officer Branton discovered a large crater in the roadway that would cause damage to any vehicle passing over it. As a result, one lane of traffic was shut down and the street was becoming congested. What would Officer Branton's best course or action be?

a) Begin directing traffic around the crater and remain there for the rest of his duty.

b) Ignore the problem, as it is not part of his duty.

c) Inform communications about the problem so that it can be fixed and leave.

d) Inform communications and his superior about the problem and remain there until action is taken to fix the crater. Have someone else monitor his post.

Question 30

You arrive on the scene of a robbery / homicide in your downtown division. There are several witnesses still present who state that the suspect fled on foot about two minutes before you arrived. They provide a brief description and direction of travel. What should your first action be?

a) Radio a description of the offending party and direction of travel for fellow officers.

b) Pursue the suspect on foot yourself.

c) Obtain complete statements from everyone at the scene

d) Seal the area off and begin collecting evidence.

Question 31

If found guilty, Kevin will be sent to jail.

No one is going to jail.

Select the logical conclusion.

a) Kevin may be found guilty tomorrow.

b) Kevin was found guilty.

c) Kevin may go to jail.

d) None of the above.

Question 32

It is generally accepted among scientists that everything that is in fact alive must breathe using some capacity.

Students completing a project found that there were no rocks that drew breathe.

Select the logical conclusion.

a) Some rocks live.

b) Everything that breathes, lives.

c) Some things that are alive, are rocks.

d) None of the above.

Question 33

There was a crime scene where none of the victims involved in the incident were found to be women.

The detective in charge of the case reported that all statements were from women.

Select the logical conclusion.

a) Some statements were from victims.

b) Some men were victims.

c) No victims gave statements.

d) None of the above.

Question 34

Susan wants to have fun so she will go with Billy to the movies. Which of the following is an assumption made in the previous statement?

a) Billy is willing to go to the movies.

b) There are movies playing.

c) Movies are fun to go to.

d) All of the above.

e) None of the above.

Question 35

The presentation has to be the best, so Jane will need to prepare a PowerPoint presentation. Which of the following is an assumption made in the previous statement?

a) Jim is not available.

b) Jane is the best presenter.

c) There are no theatres to present.

d) All of the above.

e) None of the above.

The following questions are based on the map below.

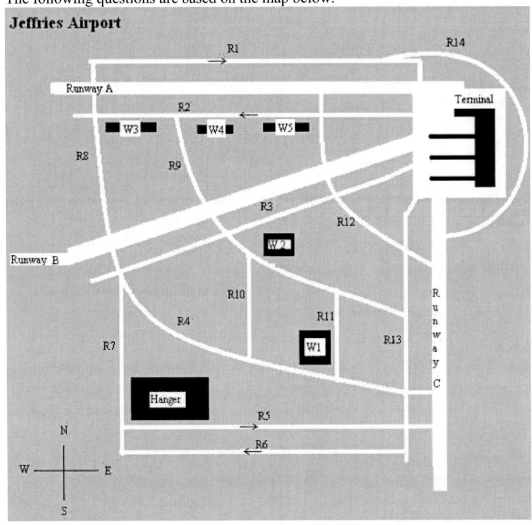

Question 36

What is the shortest route from Warehouse 1 to the Terminal?

a) R4 - R8 - R1 - the terminal.

b) R11 - R9 - R13 - the terminal.

c) R11 - R4 - R7 - R8 - R2 - the terminal.

d) R10 - R9 - the terminal.

Question 37

Which of the following statements is true?

a) R5 is a one-way road heading west.

b) Warehouse 4 is further east than warehouse 5

c) The Hanger is in the South East section of the airport.

d) The terminal is in the North East section of the airport.

Question 38

If a plane was approaching from the south, and needed to perform an emergency landing, which would be the most direct runway to land on?

a) Runway A b) Runway B

c) Runway C d) It does not matter

Question 39

Which of the following statements is false?

a) R14 connects with R1, Runway C and R12.

b) R5 is longer than R6.

c) Runway B heads in a North West direction.

d) All three runways lead off at the terminal.

Question 40

What is the quickest route from W3 to the terminal?

a) R2 - the terminal. b) R2 - R8 - R4 - R13 - the terminal.

c) R2 - R8 - R1 - the terminal. d) R2 - R9 - R3 - the terminal.

Memory Photos: You have 2 minutes to study the following picture.

Question 1
What crime was Brad Jeffersen wanted for?

a) Kidnapping   b) Drinking and Driving

c) Aggravated Assault   d) Theft

Question 2
What crime was this vehicle involved in?

a) Assault   b) Theft

c) Sexual Assault   d) Drinking and Driving

Question 3
What was Jesse Kolovak wearing?

a) Shirt and Tie   b) Checkered Shirt

c) Leather Jacket   d) Solid coloured shirt

Question 4
Which vehicle had the licence plate 306 KLM?

a) Toyota 4 Runner   b) Toyota Camry

c) Dodge Ram   d) Buick Century

Question 5
What was this suspect's identifying feature?

a) Scar upper back   b) Scar left shoulder

c) Birthmark right knee   d) Missing left index finger

Question 6

What identifying mark was on the Volkswagen Golf?

a) Missing hubcaps   b) Front hood shield

c) Rear Spoiler   d) Tinted windows

Question 7

How old was this suspect?

a) 33   b) 26   c) 30   d) 44

Question 8

Which vehicle had the licence plate 453 NMS?

a) Honda Accord   b) Dodge Ram

c) Toyota Camry   d) Toyota 4 Runner

Question 9

Who was wanted for Aggravated Assault?

a) Jesse Kolovak   b) Shane Domi

c) Brad Jeffersen   d) Narish Jamal

Question 10

How old was the person wanted for kidnapping?

a) 44   b) 33   c) 26   d) 30

Question 11

Before parking on the street which of the following conditions must be met? Answer the questions based on the by-laws studied in Book 1.

a) Must live in the house.   b) Must have oral permission.

c) Must have paid space rental.   d) Must have a compact car.

e) Must be on the grass.

Question 12

When is it acceptable to park on the grass?

a) On public holidays.   b) It is never acceptable.

c) On the weekends only.   d) After dark.

e) In the early morning.

Question 13

Who should you contact if your car is towed while parked next to the street?

a) Local garage.   b) Sheriff.

c) Mayor.   d) Girl scouts.

e) County Clerk.

Question 14

What is the punishment for parking next to the street illegally?

a) Fines.   b) Jail time.

c) Nothing.   d) Towed.

e) Public service.

Question 15

Which of the following examples is acceptable according to the by-laws?

a) Resident parks on the grass of their residence.

b) Resident parks on the curb to make room for other motorists.

c) Resident with written permission parks in front of a home they do not own.

d) Resident with verbal permission parks in front of a home they do not own.

e) Resident parks down the road from their house to mow the grass.

Question 16

If there is a car parked in front of you home without your permission you should:

a) Place a note on the car's windshield.

b) Call the appropriate authorities.

c) Bash in the windows.

d) Push the car from the front of your home.

e) Wait for the owner to come back.

Question 17

Which person does not have permission to park on the street in front of your home?

a) Neighbour   b) Son

c) Wife   d) Daughter

e) Live in mother

Question 18

Which person would be allowed to park on the street in front of your home?

a) Neighbour with verbal permission.

b) Visitor with no permission.

c) Neighbour with written permission.

d) Visitor with written permission on the grass.

e) Neighbour performing repairs on his car.

Question 19

What can happen if you park your car on the grass?

a) You will get a ticket.
b) You will be asked to move it.
c) You will get a note.
d) It will be towed.
e) It will be crushed.

Question 20

If you have gotten written permission from the owner's son, will you be allowed to park in front of the house?

a) Maybe
b) It depends on the child's age.
c) Not enough information.
d) Yes.
e) No.

Question 21

Would you be allowed to park on the curb with oral permission from the house owner?

a) No.
b) Maybe.
c) Depends on how long you will be there.
d) Not enough information.
e) Yes.

Question 22

Which following scenario would be considered unacceptable for the owner of the home per the by-laws?

a) Three cars parked in the driveway and pulled to the front.

b) Two cars parked at the front of the driveway.

c) Car parked on the street.

d) Car parked in the garage.

e) One car parked to the front of the driveway.

Question 23

How many cars can be parked in the driveway at one time?

a) 3   b) 1   c) 2   d) 5   e) 4

Question 24

When is it acceptable for a visitor to park in the driveway?

a) On weekends only.
b) Every other Sunday.
c) On holidays.
d) Anytime.
e) During the week.

Question 25

Which of the following examples is acceptable according to the bylaws?

a) Visitor parked on the grass with verbal permission.

b) Visitor parked on the street with verbal permission.

c) Visitor parked to the back of the driveway.

d) Visitor parked over the curb with written permission.

e) Visitor parked to the front of the driveway.

Answer the following according to the rules you memorized earlier.

Picture B

Picture C

Question 26

Which of the following statements is true about picture A?

a) The pots should be cleaned in the sink.

b) The sink should be running.

c) There is a coffee machine that should be full.

d) The pots should be stored in an upper cupboard.

e) None of the above.

Question 27

In picture B, which of the following is a rule being broken?

a) There is a towel on the floor that should be hanging up.

b) The lower cupboard is closed and should be opened.

c) There are pots in the lower cabinet that should be up top.

d) There is a knife on the floor.

e) None of the above.

Question 28

What is wrong in picture C?

a) There is an unclosed jar.

b) There is a pot that should be below.

c) There is a towel misplaced.

d) The toaster oven is open.

e) None of the above.

Question 29

Which pictures have a knife in an inappropriate space?

a) Picture A   b) Picture B

c) Picture C   d) Picture A and B

e) Picture A and C

Question 30

Which of the following was not a rule?

a) No food is to be left on the countertop.

b) The stove must be kept off unless cooking.

c) The coffee pot must remain full or be put away.

d) The stovetop must be kept clear of all obstacles.

e) Towels must remain hanging to dry.

Question 31

Which of the following is not a rule broken in picture B?

a) All drawers must remain closed at all times.

b) Towels must remain hanging to dry.

c) Pots must be stored in the upper cupboards.

d) The stovetop must be kept clear of all obstacles.

e) Dishes must be kept off the counter top.

Question 32

Which of the following statements is false?

a) There are parts stored in the cupboard in Picture C.

b) There is food on the counter in Picture A.

c) There is not a rule against putting dishes in the upper cupboard.

d) There is a towel hanging to dry on the stove.

e) None of the above.

Question 33

Which of the following is not a rule being broken in any of the pictures?

a) All drawers must remain closed at all times.

b) Water must not be left running.

c) Dishes must be kept off the counter top.

d) The stovetop must be kept clear of all obstacles.

e) Pots must be stored in the upper cupboards.

MEMORIZATION

The following questions are based on the picture you studied for 2 minutes.

Question 34

What flight number was delayed?

a) 227

b) 238

c) 981

d) 721

Question 35

What time was it during the event?

a) 4:30

b) 3:15

c) 1:20

d) 4:05

Question 36

What is true of the magazine the vendor was buying?

a) Eat $2.99

b) Camp $2.75

c) Fish $1.99

d) Eat $1.99

Question 37

Which of the following statements are false?

a) The child at the check in is holding a Teddy Bear.

b) The airport is in Winnipeg..

c) There are three bags being held by the customs inspector.

d) None of the above.

Question 38

What was the number on the tail of the plane above the checkout?

a) 07

b) 70

c) 67

d) None of the above.

Question 39

How many flowers were there on the bush by the arrival board?

a) 0

b) 1

c) 2

d) 3

Question 40

What was the name of the airline?

a) Nimbus Airlines

b) Nimbus Airways

c) Nimbal Airways

d) Nimbal Airlines

Question 41

What was directly below the clock on the wall?

a) Sign stating "To Terminal A"

b) Sign stating "EZ-PAY"

c) The date

d) None of the above.

Question 42

Which of the following statements is false about the security officer?

a) He is wearing a hat with a badge on it.

b) He is holding down a suspect.

c) He has a radio in his left hand.

d) None of the above.

Question 43

How many people are there by the window?

a) 1

b) 2

c) 3

d) 4

Question 44

What is the date of the event?

a) November 23.

b) November 27.

c) November 17.

d) None of the above.

Question 45

Which of the following is true about the book store?

a) The store is called Shelly's Book Nook.

b) The following magazines are displayed: Fly, Sail, Camp and Hunt..

c) There are two lights in the store.

d) All of the above.

Application For Entry

1) Child's Name

Surname	First name	Middle name (s) (optional
Smith	John	A

2) Child's Personal Information

Date of Birth	Place of Birth May 22, 2001	Height	Weight	Sex M	Date of immunization Toronto
Child's Permanent Address 123 Any Street					
Mailing Address Same					

3) Information about Parents

	Parent Applying	Other Parent
Surname (maiden name of mother)	Smith	Smith
Given name (s)	Bill	Susan
Marital Status	Married	Married
Address	123 Any Street	Same
Telephone Number		
Date of Birth	6/2/1975	
Country of Birth	Canada	

4) Legal Guardian

a) Is the child on interim or probationary adoption?   ☐ Yes   ■ No
   If yes, include a letter of authorization from the appropriate authority.

b) Who is the legal guardian of the child? _____
                                              (Name)

c) Participation of other parent – I _____ declare that I am the _____ of the child.
                                                                              (Relationship)

I acknowledge that I am aware that this application has been made and if required, I consent to the issuance of an entry in the name of the child.

                                        Bill Smith
_____   (Signature of Other Parent)
(Date)

5) Documentary Evidence of Child's Birthplace

Each time you apply for entry for your child, you must provide supporting documents. The documents will be returned. You may be requested to provide additional information or documents to confirm the child is still living in Canada.

Title of document (e.g. certificate of birth, record of birth) Birth Certificate		Date of issue 7/2/1998			
Did your child reside outside Canada before January 1, 1960? If yes, give dates for extended periods (more than 3 months).		☐ Yes	■ No		
From	To	From	To	From	To

```
Province of Ontario Canada
Name
Smith, John A.              Certificate Number
                           85-04-01124
Date of Birth
31 – 01 – 2000             Sex
                           M
Birthplace
Toronto, Ontario, Canada
                           Registration Number
Registration Date          85-04-145624
31-01-1995
                           Director
Issued On
31-03-1995
Birth Certificate
```

INSTRUCTIONS - APPLICATION FOR ENTRY

Applicants must complete the following each time they apply for entry:

- sign the application
- date the application
- submit an identification card
- include payment for the entry fee.

There is a $15 entry fee for each form processed.

CHILD'S PERSONAL INFORMATION

The entry form will be rejected if the following information is not included:
- date of birth of the child
- place of birth of the child.

LEGAL GUARDIAN OF CHILD

- Any child traveling alone must complete entry form B.
- Both parents must sign entry form B.

DOCUMENTARY EVIDENCE OF THE CHILD'S BIRTHPLACE

Documentary evidence of the child's birthplace is required if the child was born before 1960.

a) IF YOUR CHILD WAS BORN IN CANADA, you must provide a Canadian Birth Certificate

b) IF YOUR CHILD WAS BORN OUTSIDE CANADA, you must provide one of the following certificates: Certificate of Canadian Citizenship or Registration of Birth Abroad.

Question 1

Which of the following would cause the form to be refused?

a) No date of birth.

b) No middle name.

c) No parent information.

d) No parent date of birth.

e) Only one parent.

Question 2

Which of the following is an error that was made on the form?

a) Smith in surname place.   b) Marked no in legal guardian section.

c) Toronto in date of immunization place.   d) Child's street address.

e) Title of the document was left blank.

Question 3

Which section requires a signature from the applicant?

a) Child's name section.   b) Legal guardian section.

c) Child's personal information section.   d) Information about parents.

e) Child's birthplace section.

Question 4

Which of the following would cause the above form to be refused?

a) Address in wrong section.   b) Weight of child not given.

c) Date of immunization wrong.   d) No place of birth given.

e) Adoption information given.

Question 5

What is the fee associated with submission of this form?

a) 19   b) 17   c) 22   d) 25   e) 15

Question 6

What type of identification needs to be presented with this form?

a) Birth certificate.   b) Driver's license.

c) Government ID.   d) Bank statement.

e) Entry permission form.

Question 7

What additional form needs to be submitted based on an individual's situation?

a) Form A.   b) Form B.   c) Form F.

d) Form E.   e) Form L.

Question 8

Which piece of information was not put in the proper place?

a) Given name of parent applying.   b) Middle name.

c) Date of Birth.   d) Surname.

e) Sex of child.

Question 9

Which information did the applicant enter incorrectly?

a) Date of birth of parent applying.
b) Child's permanent address.
c) Given name of other parent.
d) Other parent surname.
e) Mailing address.

Question 10

Which item is not required each time the form is submitted?

a) Date of application.
b) Date of birth of parent applying.
c) Signature on the form.
d) Payment of entry fee.
e) Identification card.

Question 11

There are 4 offspring in the Yang family. They live in 6 different houses. Each offspring is married and has 3 babies. We must give 4 stuffed animals to each baby. How many stuffed animals do we need to buy?

a) 48　　　　　b) 50　　　　　c) 52　　　　　d) 54

Question 12

If there are 250 electoral vote's and they are equally divided between the 50 states, how many does each state have?

a) 4　　　　　b) 5　　　　　c) 6　　　　　d) 50

Question 13

A computer software package costs $24.07 at the local store. A customer gives 2 twenty-dollar bills. How much change does the customer receive?

a) $15.83　　　　　b) $15.93　　　　　c) $16.03　　　　　d) $16.13

Question 14

Carlene needs to save $1,440 in order to take a trip. She works 45 hours a week and earns $8 an hour. How many weeks will she have to work in order to save for the trip?

a) 3　　　　　b) 4　　　　　c) 5　　　　　d) 6

Question 15

Tim needs to fill three 20L barrels with oil. If his oil dispenser flows at 100 mL/s, how long will it take him to fill the 3 containers? (Minutes)

a) 100　　　　　b) 75　　　　　c) 50　　　　　d) 10

Question 16

The average rainfall in Waterloo has increased at an annual rate of 2%. If the total rain fall was 856mm in 2002. What is the expected rainfall in 2005? (mm)

a) 907.4　　　　　b) 908.4　　　　　c) 873.12　　　　　d) 900

Question 17

James ran 2 miles in 12 minutes. He has to run another 5 miles and wants to average a 7 minute mile over the entire run. What will James have to run the remaining 5 miles in on average to accomplish this?

a) 6.3 min / mile   b) 7.4 min / mile

c) 8.6 min / mile   d) 10.2 min / mile

Question 18

Shane and Indervir were digging a hole in the yard. They were required to remove 1000 lbs of dirt to complete the job. Shane was capable of removing 125 lbs of dirt per hour and Indervir was capable of removing 100 lbs of dirt per hour. How long would it take the two working together to complete the whole?

a) 3.45 hours   b) 4.15 hours

c) 4.45 hours   d) 5.75 hours

Question 19

A man drove for 6 hours. In that time he managed to complete 2/6 of his journey. What is the total length of his journey?

a) 18 hours   b) 20 hours

c) 24 hours   d) 30 hours

Question 20

Doug was responsible for filling out insurance requisitions at his office. In May, he was able to process 1,322 requests. In June his number of requests completed fell by 15%. In July he was able to improve on his June numbers by 17%. How many requisitions did Doug complete in July?

a) 1,300   b) 1,315   c) 1,348   d) 1,412

Identify the spelling errors in the following questions.

Question 21

Despite many complaints and concerns <u>from citizens</u>, the instances of <u>retaliation for</u> testifying in court are very rare. Despite this <u>rarety</u>, officers should be vigilant of suspects <u>who</u> attempt to intimidate witnesses.

a) rarety   b) retaliation for

c) from citizens   d) who

Question 22

The rookie officers <u>undertook</u> extensive training and development programs in order to prepare them for the <u>daunting</u> tasks that would lie <u>ahead</u> of them as they <u>commensed</u> their duties.

a) undertook   b) daunting

c) lie ahead   d) commensed

Question 23

The viscious canine attacked the young woman and her sibling. When animal control arrived they managed to subdue the animal through tranquilizers and harnesses.

a) viscious   b) sibling

c) subdue   d) tranquilizers

Question 24

There were thousands of demonstrators at Parliament Hill protesting the atrocities of foriegn governments with horrible human rights records.

a) demonstrators   b) atrocities

c) foriegn   d) horrible

Question 25

Psychology, sociology and criminalogy are several examples of courses that can be taken at university which help prepare students for a potential career in policing.

a) Psychology   b) sociology

c) criminalogy   d) potential

Question 26

Unions are increasingly becoming involved in local politics. They have started supporting particular political campains. This has caused some controversy, as there are several groups who feel the unions should remain apolitical.

a) increasingly   b) campains

c) controversy   d) apolitical

Question 27

Because security officers are forced to work both day and night shifts, it is important that they maintain a healthy diet and exercise regime. If they do not receive enough nurishment, physical activity and rest, they will have difficulty performing their jobs. Officers sometimes complain that they have become nocturnal creatures like bats.

a) regime   b) nurishment

c) receive   d) nocturnal

Question 28

Coup means:

a) Chicken's Home   b) Rebellion

c) Large Cup   d) Shelter

Question 29

Indirect means:

a) Oblique   b) Unique

c) Differentiated   d) Rare

Question 30
Incarcerate means:
a) Charge
b) Determine Guilt
c) Arrest
d) Imprison

Question 31
Diffident means:
a) Timid
b) Brash
c) Ardent
d) Difficult

Question 32
Sheltered means:
a) Enveloped
b) Nursed
c) Protected
d) Forgotten

Question 33
Axis means:
a) Hinge
b) Admission
c) Partnership
d) Deal

Question 34
Dogmatic means:
a) Moderate
b) Dictatorial
c) Dog Shampoo
d) Theoretical

Question 35
Frail means:
a) Not Pass
b) Sash
c) Quill
d) Fragile

Question 36
Submissive means:
a) Passive
b) Quiet
c) Quaint
d) Eloquent

Question 37
Violate means:
a) Allow
b) Deny
c) Contravene
d) Ignore

Question 38

Indicate which underlined portion contains an error in the following questions. The suspect fled <u>into the street</u> then turned a corner <u>quickly</u>. It was better that he fled <u>rather then</u> staying in the bank and taking <u>hostages</u>.

a) into the street   b) quickly

c) rather then   d) hostages

Question 39

"<u>Who</u> cares whether old people <u>can</u> take care of <u>theirselves</u> or not?" asked the young college student as <u>he prepared</u> for his psychology exam.

a) Who   b) can

c) theirselves   d) he prepared

Question 40

The <u>collision</u> happened <u>on account of</u> the brakes were faulty. Had the brakes been <u>functioning</u> properly <u>then</u> she would have been able to stop.

a) happened   b) on account of

c) functioning   d) then

Question 41

I am <u>extremely</u> impressed <u>with your</u> dedication. Since you began <u>training; you</u> have been <u>able to work</u> the entire shift without rest.

a) extremely   b) with your

c) training; you   d) able to work

Question 42

<u>Because</u> she had been married <u>twice</u>, she had two <u>mothers-in-law</u> in her life. She <u>didn't like neither</u>.

a) Because   b) twice

c) mothers-in-law   d) didn't like neither

Question 43

A recent <u>New York University</u> study <u>show</u> that cancer is <u>more prevalent</u> in California <u>than</u> on the east coast.

a) New York University   b) show

c) more prevalent   d) than

Answer the following questions based on the passage below.

Harassment Complaint Report

On January 3, 2001 Janet Brinkman came to my office to report an incident of sexual harassment. She alleged that Isaac Reynolds proposed sexual relations with her at the New Year's Party in the office. He also fondled her and tried to unbutton her shirt.

I called Isaac Reynolds into my office to discuss the allegations on January 4, 2001. Mr. Reynolds said that Ms. Brinkman was intoxicated and dancing on the desks at the party. He offered to help her down so she would not stumble and injure herself. When she was climbing down she did stumble and Mr. Reynolds accidentally touched her breast. He said that he did not make any comments to Ms. Brinkman other than to be careful and stay off of the desks.

I documented the report and the reply on company forms. I presented the forms to the human resource department on January 10, 2001. I gave an oral summary of what I was told by both employees. I could not give an impression of which person was telling the true events of the party. I could offer that I know that Mr. Reynolds does not drink due to being a recovering alcoholic.

The department heads reviewed the forms and re-interviewed Ms. Brinkman and Mr. Reynolds. They made a decision based on the evidence that there was no harassment that night in question.

Question 44

Who initially filed the report of sexual harassment?

a) Janet Brinkman.   b) Lesley Reynolds.

c) Lisa Simmons.   d) Carley William.

e) Sharon Newman.

Question 45

Why did Ms. Brinkman stumble at the party?

a) She had been drinking.   b) She was tired.

c) She was dizzy from spinning.   d) Someone pushed her.

e) She was sick.

Question 46

What was Mr. Reynolds accused of doing?

a) Proposing sexual relations with everyone at the party.

b) Exposing himself to a woman giving him a ride home.

c) Fondling a woman and trying to unbutton her shirt.

d) Walking into the woman's dressing room while it was occupied.

e) Walking around in his underwear in front of the staff.

Question 47

When was the report completed and handed over to the human resource department?

a) 10-Jan-01   b) 10-Feb-01

c) 10-Aug-01   d) 10-Dec-01

e) 10-Jul-01

Question 48

What reason did the manager offer to the department heads for why Mr. Reynolds was more than likely not drinking that night?

a) He is an all around nice guy.

b) He is unable to handle his liquor.

c) He has never been in trouble before.

d) He is remorseful about the incident.

e) He is a recovering alcoholic.

Answer the following questions based on the passage below.

Seizure Report

On August 17, 2004 a personal package from Peru was sent to my office for review. The package was a box that was not very large. It had a liquid stain of some sort on one corner and was marked "fragile". When I contacted the addressee, Jacob Michaels, he declared he had no knowledge of a package coming from Peru. The address information however was correct on the packaging.

When the package was opened, inside were small medicine type bottles with no labels. The liquid was sent to the lab on September 1, 2004. It was determined to be liquid cocaine. Mr. Michael was brought in for questioning on September 20, 2004 since all of the information on the packaging was correct.

Mr. Michaels informed me that he was in the middle of a bitter divorce. His wife has tried to frame him in the past for other petty crimes. In light of this information, I decided to contact the person who mailed the package.

Due to a lack of extrication laws, Mr. Gonzales was more than willing to speak with me about the package. He told me that it was a woman who had ordered the cocaine and had it sent in a man's name. On October 15, 2004 I contacted Mr. Michael's wife and she confessed to ordering the cocaine and having it sent to Mr. Michael's home. It was determined that she would not get custody of her children and would have to pay a $1,500 fine.

Question 49

What seems to be the motivation for the crime?

a) Revenge due to a bitter relationship.

b) Money making scheme.

c) Deviant behaviour is irresistible.

d) Inability to break away from the illegal lifestyle.

e) Being forced into the business.

Question 50

Where did the package originate?

a) United States.

b) Peru.

c) Chile.

d) Mexico.

e) Columbia.

Question 51

What was Mr. Michael's response about the package?

a) He had ordered something larger from Peru.

b) He ordered a musical globe from Mexico.

c) His children were pen pals with children from other countries.

d) His wife must have ordered the item.

e) He had no knowledge of the package.

Question 52

Who led the police to Mr. Michaels's wife?

a) Mr. Griffin.

b) Mr. Michaels.

c) Mr. Wentworth.

d) Mr. Gonzales.

e) Mr. Kingston.

Question 53

What was the penalty for the guilty party in this case?

a) Jailed for 5 years and fined $2,000.

b) Lost custody of the children and jailed for 15 years.

c) Jailed for 2 years and assigned 80 hours of community service.

d) Fined $2,000 and assigned 40 hours of community service.

e) Lost custody of the children and fined $1,500.

Answer the following questions based on the information below.
Application for Food Stamps

YOUR NAME (First, Middle, Last) Willie Jones	Birth date (Mo., Day, Yr.) 7/1/72	Social Security Number 7/1/72

Mailing Address 123 Anywhere Street		Street Address, if different n/a	
City Anywhere	State Michigan	Zip 03741	Telephone/Message Number during the day (237)-555-1469-7

Expedited Services

You may be able to receive food stamps benefits within 5 calendar days if: your food stamp household has less than $150 in monthly gross income and liquid assets, or if your rent payment exceeds your household's combined monthly income.

1. How much money do the members of your household have in cash or a bank account?
_____$300_____
2. What is the total amount of income your household expects to receive this month?
_____$700/year_____
3. What is your current monthly rent payment? $___$459_____ Utilities? $__$350_____
4. Is anyone in the household a migrant or farm worker? ____no_____

In accordance with Federal Law and Regulation a person cannot be denied benefits based on race, color, religion, national origin, sex, or disability.

Penalty Warnings and Perjury Statement

When your household receives food stamps benefits, your household must follow all of the rules set forth by this office. Any member who breaks the rules can be disallowed benefits for up to one full year, be fined up to $250,000 and may face time in prison. The rules are as follows:

- Do not trade or sell food stamp benefits or EBT cards
- Do not use someone else's food stamp benefits, identification card, or EBT card for yourself
- Do not give false information or hide information to get or continue to get food stamps.

I certify that under penalty of perjury that my answers to all questions about each household member are correct and complete.

William Jones
Primary Applicant Signature   Date May 10, 2000

Identification

Social Security Card 342-678-4421 William Jones

Social Security Card 966-67-8903 Beatrice Smith

Applicants must complete the following each time they apply:

- include the full name of the applicant
- submit an identification card
- sign the application
- include the amount of income expected in the next month

There is no fee to process the form.

Personal Information

The application will be rejected if the following information is not included:
- full name
- social security number

Expedited Services

Total rent payment needs to be given.

Utility amount should not include any phone charges.

Penalty Warnings and Perjury Statement

Only the primary applicant needs to sign the form.

If currently employed you must submit a Form E with the application.

Question 54

Which of the following would cause the above form to be refused?

a) The money in cash and accounts question is not answered.

b) The rent payment is not given.

c) The state of residence is not included.

d) The date of birth is not included.

e) The social security number is not included.

Question 55

Which of the following is an error that was made on the form?

a) Mailing address not entered in.

b) State is spelled incorrectly.

c) Zip code entered incorrectly.

d) Utilities are not given in a dollar amount.

e) None of the above.

Question 56

Which section requires a signature from the applicant?

a) Expedited services section.

b) Name section.

c) Penalty Warnings and Perjury Statement section.

d) Address information section.

e) Application deadline section.

Question 57

Which of the following would cause a form to be refused?

a) Total rent payment not entered.   b) The social security number is missing.

c) There is no date on the form.   d) Form E is included.

e) There are no migrant farm workers.

Question 58
What is the fee associated with submission of this form?

a) No fee.   b) 5   c) 10

d) 15   e) 20

Question 59
What type of identification needs to be presented with this form?

a) Driver's license.   b) Government ID.

c) Social security card.   d) Birth certificate.

e) Food handler's card.

Question 60
What additional form needs to be submitted based on an individual's situation?

a) Eligibility addendum.   b) Bank holdings addendum.

c) Relationship addendum. d) Employment addendum.

e) Utilities addendum.

Question 61
Which piece of information was not put in the proper place?

a) Cash in bank   b) Date of birth.   c) Applicant name.

d) State.   e) Zip code.

Question 62
Which information did the applicant enter incorrectly?

a) Current rent payment.   b) State of residence.

c) Total income for the next month.   d) Birth date.

e) Total utilities payment.

Question 63
Which item is not required each time the form is submitted?

a) Full applicant name.   b) Identification card.

c) Signature on the form.   d) Amount of money on hand.

e) Amount of income expected in the next month.

Question 64
Kent put change in a bottle. He put in 3 pennies, 6 quarters, 3 dimes and 1 nickel. What is the probability of picking out a quarter?

a) 23 %   b) 8 %   c) 33 %   d) 46 %

Question 65

A computer software package costs $27.91 at the local store. A customer gives 3 ten-dollar bills. How much change does the customer receive?

a) $1.89   b) $1.95   c) $2.09   d) $2.15

Question 66

Kevin determined that he could ski at the rate of 6 m in 1/5 of a second. How many meters could Kevin ski in 12 seconds?

a) 360 m   b) 380 m   c) 400 m   d) 420 m

Question 67

Simon studied longer than Shelley, but not as long as Kate. Shelley did all of her studying with Claire. Claire then studied with Kate. Who did the least studying?

a) Kate   b) Claire   c) Simon   d) Shelley

Question 68

The perimeter of a square is 20 meters. Which of the following is the area of the square?

a) 28 metres squared   b) 40 metres squared

c) 240 metres squared   d) none of these

Identify which of the following words is misspelled.

Question 69

a) ability   b) staple   c) compatible

d) specifically   e) None of the above

Question 70

a) corruption   b) withdrawal   c) unnecesary

d) disappearance   e) None of the above

Question 71

a) disability   b) fruadulent   c) gradually

d) university   e) None of the above

Question 72

a) rehabilitation   b) grasping   c) progresion

d) negotiable   e) None of the above

Question 73

a) front   b) government   c) implication

d) inspector   e) None of the above

Question 74

a) Incapabel   b) honesty   c) fulfilment
d) engagement   e) None of the above

Question 75

a) distressed   b) whisper   c) vocale
d) licensing   e) None of the above

Fill in the blanks with the most appropriate word.

Question 76

Due to the size of the _____, Billy had to put on his glasses to read the letter.

a) paper   b) print   c) pencil   d) sun

Question 77

In science class James learned that rapid cell growth is called _____.

a) proliferation   b) progression   c) proteination   d) protection

Question 78

In the Middle Ages many sieges were won when a _____ was used to throw large stones like missiles.

a) pistol   b) catapult   c) shotgun   d) slingshot

Question 79

The type of evergreen with small white flowers is called a _____.

a) daffodil   b) rag wood   c) juniper   d) pine tree

Question 80

The young officer was so _____ that he had no problem getting information from the female perpetrators.

a) gallant   b) inhibited   c) passive   d) timid

Indicate which underlined portions contain an error.
Question 81

Several noise <u>complaint originated</u> from a <u>celebration during</u> a street festival promoting jazz music. Noise levels that <u>persisted past</u> 3:00 in the morning infuriated citizens <u>who live</u> in the neighbourhood.

a) complaint originated   b) celebration during
c) persisted past   d) who live

Question 82

Of his three brothers, Jamal was the stronger. He could bench press at least 50 pounds more than his nearest sibling.

a) Of his   b) was the stronger

c) at least   d) more than

Question 83

She couldn't have been more happier on her wedding day, even if she had married in Hawaii.

a) couldn't have   b) more happier

c) day, even   d) had married

Question 84

My younger brother doesn't have a job right now. Currently he is hoping his quickly typing skills will land him a temporary job.

a) doesn't   b) Currently

c) quickly   d) would land

Indicate any punctuation errors in the sentences below:

Question 85

Before taking the tickets, the teenager must clock in, then she can begin work.

a) taking   b) in, then   c) can

d) work.   e) No correction required

Question 86

When planning an outing with children, remember to bring: activities, snacks, and a first aid kit.

a) children,   b) bring: c) , snacks, and a

d) aid kit.   e) No correction required

Answer the following questions based on what is stated or implied in the following passages.

Question 87

While performing a search on a person that is under arrest you should follow the steps below.

> 1) Handcuff the prisoner behind the back
> 2) Search the area around the suspect's hands
> 3) Ask the suspect if he has anything in his pockets
> 3) Look in the suspect's pockets
> 4) Feel the suspect's pockets with a bar or pen
> 5) Crimp the pocket with your hand
> 6) Reach into the pocket and remove any objects very carefully

What is the last step that is taken by an officer performing a search on a prisoner?

a) Visual contact

b) Contact through a tool or instrument

c) Direct physical contact with an object

d) Physical contact through the clothing

Question 88

During the course of your training you are taught the procedures you should follow when you encounter a major accident scene, or dangerous situation.

> 1) Get appropriate backup and emergency personnel en route to assist you
> 2) Create a safe work environment to perform your duties
> 3) Assist people in immediate life threatening situations
> 4) Treat victims in order of emergency priority
> 5) Transport victims in need of medical attention to the hospital
> 6) Collect evidence on scene
> 7) Clear the area for normal use

Which of the following is the most important step to take when you arrive at an emergency scene?

a) Transport injured parties to the hospital

b) Treat an injured woman who is bleeding from her head

c) Assist a man who is trapped in a vehicle, which is on fire

d) Preserve evidence proving that the driver was under the influence of alcohol

Question 89

While parading a prisoner before the officer in charge (OIC) of a station the following actions have to be taken by the arresting officer:

      1) Identify the arrested party
      2) Explain the reason for the arrest
      3) Inform the OIC that the accused has been read his rights to counsel
      4) Explain why the accused needed to be brought to the station
      5) Identify any medical conditions the accused has
      6) Identify any money or valuable property the accused has

An officer walks into the station with a prisoner and explains that he is under arrest for assault and brought back to the station to prevent further offences from occurring. Which steps are missing?

a) The suspect's name, age, medical condition and any valuables the prisoner has

b) The prisoner's name, medical condition, list of valuables, and that he has been read his rights to counsel

c) The prisoner's age, medical condition and list of valuable property

d) Both A and B

Question 90

While investigating an alarm call the following steps have to be taken:

      1) Attend the residence
      2) Visually and physically check all points of entry to ensure they are secure
      3) If you find an insecure premise establish a perimeter around the building
      4) Call for back up
      5) Notify a road supervisor
      6) Enter the building and do a room by room search
      7) Notify the alarm company and owner of the building

You are dispatched to an alarm call with your road supervisor at a local YMCA. When you arrive you can see that a window has been broken. Which steps should you take next?

a) Establish a perimeter around the building.

b) Call for back up

c) Perform a search of the building

d) All of the above

Book 2

1) D	11) A	21) C	31) D
2) B	12) C	22) C	32) D
3) C	13) B	23) D	33) C
4) A	14) D	24) B	34) D
5) C	15) C	25) C	35) B
6) A	16) C	26) A	36) B
7) C	17) A	27) C	37) D
8) B	18) C	28) B	38) C
9) D	19) B	29) D	39) A
10) B	20) A	30) A	40) C

10/10   9/10   5/5

Book 4

1) B	16) B	31) C
2) C	17) A	32) A
3) A	18) C	33) B
4) A	19) D	34) B
5) D	20) E	35) D
6) B	21) A	36) A
7) C	22) A	37) C
8) A	23) C	38) A
9) D	24) D	39) D
10) B	25) E	40) B
11) A	26) D	41) A
12) B	27) A	42) C
13) E	28) E	43) B
14) D	29) D	44) A
15) C	30) C	45) D

11/15   13/15   8/15

55/70

Book 5

1) A	16) B	31) A
2) C	17) B	32) C
3) B	18) C	33) C
4) D	19) A	34) B
5) E	20) B	35) D
6) A	21) A	36) A
7) B	22) D	37) C
8) C	23) A	38) C
9) D	24) C	39) C
10) B	25) C	40) B
11) A	26) B	41) C
12) B	27) B	42) D
13) B	28) B	43) B
14) B	29) A	44) A
15) D	30) D	45) A

46) C	61) B	76) B
47) A	62) C	77) A
48) E	63) D	78) B
49) A	64) D	79) C
50) B	65) C	80) A
51) E	66) A	81) A
52) D	67) D	82) B
53) E	68) D	83) B
54) E	69) E	84) C
55) E	70) C	85) B
56) C	71) B	86) B
57) B	72) C	87) C
58) A	73) E	88) C
59) C	74) A	89) B
60) D	75) C	90) D

Book 2 (Questions 1 – 5 review answer sheet)

Question 6

A – Same   B - Tighter Hexagon

C - Smaller Star   D - Knick on bottom

Question 7

A - Wider Hexagon   B - Thicker top spike

C – Same   D - No white space on left side

Question 8

A - No space above heart   B - Same

C - Circle rotated slightly   D - Thin middle square

Question 9

A - Thinner circle   B - Thick box

C - Line bottom right   D - Same

Question 10

A - White spot   B - Same

C – Larger nose   D - Missing tooth

Question 11

A – Same   B - Extra Tooth

C – Extra black line on right side   D – Left ear more black

Question 12

A - Smaller nose   B - Smaller Reign

C - Same   D - Bigger ear

Question 13

A - Bump on back   B - Same

C - Line temple   D - No bump ear

Question 14

A – Thinner   B - No point willow

C - White line grass   D - Same

Question 15

A - White on wing   B - Fatter

C - Same   D – Shorter

(Questions 16 – 25 review answer sheet)

Question 26

Concern for safety is one of the key competencies for being an officer. Approaching a large group with very little information alone can be dangerous. Groups would be more cooperative with two officers and if something should happen, an additional officer would be available.

Question 27

Concern for safety is one of the key competencies for being an officer. This is not an emergency situation and there is no need to rush into the situation.

Question 28

Assertiveness is one of the core competencies of being an officer. There is nothing wrong with telling individuals to keep their hands where they are visible for officer safety reasons. You have no legal authority to search any of the individuals in the park at this time.

Question 29

Officer Branton would have to inform his supervisor about his actions to ensure that his patrol is covered. The traffic problem has to be dealt with as well.

Question 30

You must make an effort to capture the suspect. The best means of doing this is to get a description of the suspects out immediately.

(Question 31 – 33 review answer sheet)

Question 34

There are three assumptions made.
1) Billy is willing to attend.

2) It is possible to attend the movies.
3) Movies are fun.

Question 35

The only assumption made is that Jane is the best presenter available, otherwise someone else would be selected. There is no assumption made about the suitability of other presenters, or of the ability to present in different locations.

(Questions 36 – 40 review answer sheet)
Book 4

Review the answer sheet.

Book 5

(Questions 1 – 10 review answer sheet)

Question 11

There are a total of 12 babies (4 x 3 = 12). If each one has 4 toys, there are a total of 48 toys (12 x 4 = 48).

Question 12

Each state will have 5 votes (250 / 50 = 5).

Question 13

The customer gave the store $40 (2 x 20 = 40). The change the customer received was $15.93 (40.00 – 24.07 = $15.93).

Question 14

Carlene makes $360 per week (45 x $8 = $360). It would therefore require 4 weeks to save for the trip (1440 / 360 = 4).

Question 15

First determine volume of three containers [3 x 20L = 60L]. Then convert fill rate from mL/s to L/min. Recall 1L = 1000mL and 60s = 1 minute; [100 / 1000 x 60 = 6L/min]; Then divide total volume by fill rate [60 / 6 = 10 minutes]

Question 16

The annual increase in rain fall from one year to the next is 2%. Starting at 856mm (2002), begin to calculate the rainfall for the following years: 856 x 1.02 = 873.12mm (2003); then 873.12 x 1.02 = 890.58mm (2004); finally, 890.58 x 1.02 = 908.4 mm (2005).

Question 17

There are two components to the run: the 2 miles at 6 minutes/mile (12 / 2 = 6) and the 5 miles at "y" minutes/mile. When these two numbers are added together and divided by 7, the result must be 7.

$$\frac{2(6) + 5(y)}{7} = 7 \qquad\qquad \frac{12 + 5(y)}{7} = 7$$

$$7 \times \frac{12 + 5(y)}{7} = 7 \times 7 \qquad\qquad 12 + 5(y) = 49$$

$$12 - 12 + 5y = 49 - 12 \qquad\qquad 5(y) = 37$$

$$5(y) / 5 = 37 / 5 \qquad\qquad y = 7.4 \text{ minutes / mile}$$

Question 18

Shane and Indervir can remove 225 lbs / hour when they work together (100 + 125 = 225). To remove 1000 lbs of dirt, they would have to work for 4.45 hours (1000 / 225 = 4.44 hours). You have to round up in this type of question.

Question 19

The 6 hours completed represents 2/6 of the journey. To determine the entire trip, you have to multiply the part of the trip completed to the denominator (bottom portion of the fraction) and then divide by the numerator (top portion of the fraction). This results in the total length of the trip of 18 hours. (6 x 6 / 2 = 18).

Question 20

Doug processed 1,124 requests in June (1322 x 0.85 = 1124). In July he processed 1,315 requests (1124 x 1.17).

Question 21

Rarety should be spelled rarity.

Question 22

Commensed should be spelled commenced.

Question 23

Viscious should be spelled vicious.

Question 24

Foriegn should be spelled foreign.

Question 25

Criminalogy should be spelled criminology.

Question 26

Campains should be spelled campaigns.

Question 27

Nuishment should be spelled nourishment.

(Questions 28 – 37 review answer sheet)

Question 38

"Rather then" is an incorrect use of language. The word "then" is used for instances of time (I will put on my sleeping garments and then get into bed). The correct term would be "rather than", which is used when making comparisons.

Question 39

There is no such word as "theirselves". The correct word would be "themselves".

Question 40

"On account of" is improper use of the language. The correct word that should be used in this situation is "because".

Question 41

A semicolon is used to separate independent clauses. An independent clause can stand alone as a complete sentence. In this case the clause "Since you began training" could not stand as an independent clause. Because of this, a semicolon is inappropriate punctuation. It should be removed.

Question 42

The phrase "didn't like neither" contains a double negative and is confusing. The phrase should be written "didn't like either".

Question 43

The above sentence has a problem with subject / verb agreement. The verb "show" (plural form) should agree with the subject of the sentence "study". The sentence should read: A recent New York University study shows that …

(Questions 44 – 63 review answer sheet)

Question 64

There are a total of 13 coins (3 + 6 + 3 + 1 = 13). This means there is a 46.1% chance of pulling out a quarter (6 / 13 = 46.1%).

Question 65

The customer receives $2.09 change ($30.00 – 27.91 = $2.09).

Question 66

Kevin can ski 30 meters in 1 second (6 x 5 = 30). In 12 seconds, he can ski 360 metres (12 x 30 = 360).

Question 67

You will have to rank the information.

First Sentence: Kate   **Second Sentence:**   Shelly - Claire
                             Simon
                             Shelley

Third Sentence: Claire does more studying than Shelley. Therefore Shelley does the least amount of studying.

Question 68

Area of a square or rectangle = length x width

Perimeter of a square or rectangle = (length + width) x 2

(Question 69 – 75 review answer sheet)

Question 76

"Print" is the correct answer. The size of the letters was too small to read.

Question 77

Proliferation is the correct answer. It means propagation, creation or production.

Question 78

A "catapult" is an older weapon that flung large rocks like missiles.

Question 79

A "daffodil" is a small flower, "rag wood" is a weed and a "pine tree" does not have flowers. The correct answer is "juniper".

Question 80

"Gallant" is the correct answer. It means brave or courageous.

Question 81

Complaint should be plural as there were "several" of them. The sentence should read: Several noise complaints originated…

Question 82

When there are more than two objects or people being compared, you must use a "est" ending, in this case, "strongest". "Stronger" should only be used for comparing two different people or objects.

Question 83

For comparative adjectives and adverbs, if the word has multiple syllables then you must use the modifying word more or most as opposed to adding the –er / -est ending. You cannot do both. The sentence should read: "She couldn't have been more happy …"

Question 84

The word "quickly" is an adverb that is describing a noun ("skills" not "typing"). The adjective form of the word should be used (quick). The sentence should therefore read:" … he was hoping his quick typing skills…"

Question 85

A period is required after the word "in"; otherwise, a run-on sentence is created.

Question 86

A colon should not be used before a series introduced by a verb or preposition.

(Question 87 – 90 review answer sheet.)

eCFAT

The electronic Canadian Forces Aptitude Test (eCFAT) is used to help determine specific Military Occupations for which you are best suited. There are three components to the test.
- · Verbal Skills - 15 questions / 5 minutes
- · Spatial Ability - 15 questions / 10 minutes
- · Problem Solving - 30 questions / 30 minutes

Only paper, pencils and erasers are allowed - no books, dictionaries, notes, writing paper, calculators, calculator watches or other aids are permitted in the room.

Detach the answer sheet to take the test.

Answer Sheet eCFAT

Verbal Test

	A	B	C	D	
1)	○	○	○	○	_____
2)	○	○	○	○	_____
3)	○	○	○	○	_____
4)	○	○	○	○	_____
5)	○	○	○	○	_____
6)	○	○	○	○	_____
7)	○	○	○	○	_____
8)	○	○	○	○	_____

	A	B	C	D	E	F	
9)	○	○	○	○	○	○	_____
10)	○	○	○	○	○	○	_____
11)	○	○	○	○	○	○	_____
12)	○	○	○	○	○	○	_____
13)	○	○	○	○	○	○	_____
14)	○	○	○	○	○	○	_____
15)	○	○	○	○	○	○	_____

Total _____ / 15

Spatial Test

	A	B	C	D	
1)	○	○	○	○	_____
2)	○	○	○	○	_____
3)	○	○	○	○	_____
4)	○	○	○	○	_____
5)	○	○	○	○	_____
6)	○	○	○	○	_____
7)	○	○	○	○	_____
8)	○	○	○	○	_____
9)	○	○	○	○	_____
10)	○	○	○	○	_____
11)	○	○	○	○	_____
12)	○	○	○	○	_____

	A	B	C	D	
13)	○	○	○	○	_____
14)	○	○	○	○	_____
15)	○	○	○	○	_____
16)	○	○	○	○	_____
17)	○	○	○	○	_____
18)	○	○	○	○	_____
19)	○	○	○	○	_____
20)	○	○	○	○	_____
21)	○	○	○	○	_____
22)	○	○	○	○	_____
23)	○	○	○	○	_____
24)	○	○	○	○	_____

	A	B	C	D	
25)	○	○	○	○	_____
26)	○	○	○	○	_____
27)	○	○	○	○	_____
28)	○	○	○	○	_____
29)	○	○	○	○	_____
30)	○	○	○	○	_____
31)	○	○	○	○	_____
32)	○	○	○	○	_____
33)	○	○	○	○	_____
34)	○	○	○	○	_____
35)	○	○	○	○	_____

Total _____ / 35

Problem Solving Test

	A	B	C	D	E	F	
1)	○	○	○	○			_____
2)	○	○	○	○			_____
3)	○	○	○	○			_____
4)	○	○	○	○	E	F	_____
5)	○	○	○	○	○	○	_____
6)	○	○	○	○	○	○	_____
7)	○	○	○	○	○	○	_____
8)	○	○	○	○	○	○	_____
9)	○	○	○	○	○	○	_____
10)	○	○	○	○			_____

	A	B	C	D	
11)	○	○	○	○	_____
12)	○	○	○	○	_____
13)	○	○	○	○	_____
14)	○	○	○	○	_____
15)	○	○	○	○	_____
16)	○	○	○	○	_____
17)	○	○	○	○	_____
18)	○	○	○	○	_____
19)	○	○	○	○	_____
20)	○	○	○	○	_____

	A	B	C	D	
21)	○	○	○	○	_____
22)	○	○	○	○	_____
23)	○	○	○	○	_____
24)	○	○	○	○	_____
25)	○	○	○	○	_____
26)	○	○	○	○	_____
27)	○	○	○	○	_____
28)	○	○	○	○	_____
29)	○	○	○	○	_____
30)	○	○	○	○	_____

Total _____ / 30   **Total _____ / 80**

Question 1

Expendable means:

a) Able to Grow   b) Disposable

c) Careful   d) Watchful

Question 2

Abominable means:

a) Hateful   b) Snowman

c) Violent   d) A bomb

Question 3

Mystique means:

a) Foggy   b) Air of Mystery

c) Failed   d) Began

Question 4

Commenced means:

a) Finished   b) Graduation

c) Failed   d) Began

Question 5

Daunting means:

a) Extensive   b) Developed

c) Charming   d) Discouraging

Question 6

Pigment means:

a) Colouring Agent   b) Young Pig

c) Stupid   d) Stubborn

Question 7

Forlorn means:

a) Worn Out   b) Joyful

c) Dejected   d) Grassy Quadrangle

Question 8

Vicious means:

a) Sticky   b) Ferocious

c) Short   d) Fast

Question 9

Which two words have the opposite meaning?
a) Credible   b) Untrustworthy   c) Challenging   d) Careful

a) a & b   b) a & c   c) a & d
d) b & c   e) b & d   f) c & d

Question 10

Which two words have the opposite meaning?
a) Opposite   b) Premature   c) Alike   d) Gentle

a) a & b   b) a & c   c) a & d
d) b & c   e) b & d   f) c & d

Question 11

Which two words have the opposite meaning?
a) Grant   b) Praise   c) Condemn   d) Harden

a) a & b   b) a & c   c) a & d
d) b & c   e) b & d   f) c & d

Question 12

Which two words have the opposite meaning?
a) Replenish   b) Reuse   c) Empty   d) Taint

a) a & b   b) a & c   c) a & d
d) b & c   e) b & d   f) c & d

Question 13

Which two words have the same meaning?
a) Strong   b) Harmful   c) Frail   d) Delicate

a) a & b   b) a & c   c) a & d
d) b & c   e) b & d   f) c & d

Question 14

Which two words have the same meaning?
a) Toil   b) Enigma   c) Grow   d) Labour

a) a & b   b) a & c   c) a & d
d) b & c   e) b & d   f) c & d

Question 15

Which two words have the opposite meaning?
a) Tall   b) Wide   c) Large   d) Narrow

a) a & b   b) a & c   c) a & d
d) b & c   e) b & d   f) c & d

Question 1

A   B   C   D

Question 2

A   B   C   D

Question 3

A   B   C   D

Question 4

A   B   C   D

Question 5

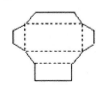

A   B   C   D

Question 6

A   B   C   D

Question 7

A   B   C   D

Question 8

A   B   C   D

Question 9

A   R   C   D

Question 10

A   B   C   D

Question 11

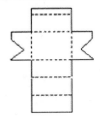

A   B   C   D

Question 12

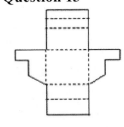

A   B   C   D

Question 13

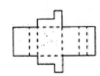

A   B   C   D

Question 14

A   B   C   D

Question 15

A   B   C   D

Question 16

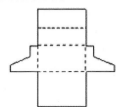 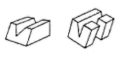 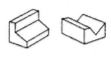

A   B   C   D

Question 17

 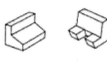

A   B   C   D

Question 18

A   B   C   D

Question 19

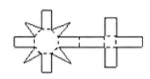

A   B   C   D

Question 20

A   B   C   D

Question 21

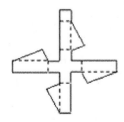

A   B   C   D

Question 22

A   B   C   D

Question 23

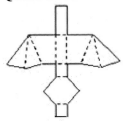

A   B   C   D

Question 24

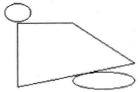

A   B   C   D

Question 25

A   B   C   D

Question 26

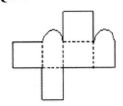

A   B   C   D

Question 27

    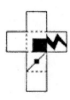

A   B   C   D

Question 28

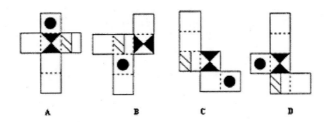

A   B   C   D

Question 29

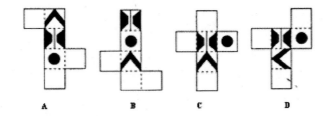

A   B   C   D

Question 30

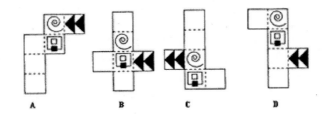

A   B   C   D

Question 31

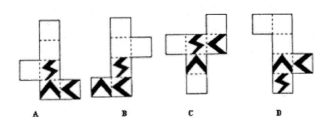

A   B   C   D

Question 32

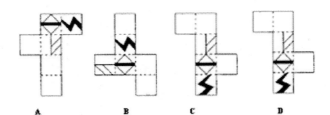

A   B   C   D

Question 33

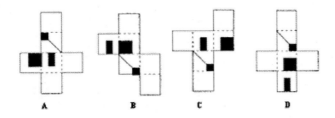

A   B   C   D

Question 34

    A   **B**   **C**   **D**

Question 35

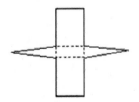

    A   **B**   **C**   **D**

Question 1

521 x 346 =

a) 123 566   b) 150 326   c) 180 266   d) none of these

Question 2

What time is it in Toronto when it is 1 pm Eastern Standard time in Melbourne? Melbourne time is 16 hours ahead of Toronto's time.

a) 9 pm   b) 9 am   c) 7 am   d) 7 pm

Question 3

How much change would James receive after paying $50.00 for the following products:

         6 packets of crackers at $3.54 a packet
         5 kg of oranges at $1.95 a kilogram
         3 dozen muffins at $3.75 per dozen

a) $42.24   b) $24.16   c) $7.76   d) none of these

Question 4

Which of the following represents fractions arranged in a decreasing order of size?

a) 0.003, 0.02, 0.1   b) 2/3, 1/4, 13/15, 3/5, 5/1

c) 15/16, 7/8, 3/4, 2/3, ½   d) none of the above

Which is the missing image in the patterns below?
Question 5

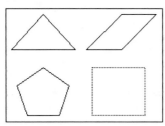

a)   b)   c)

d)   e)   f)

Question 6

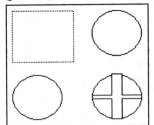

 a)

 b)

 c)

 d)

 e)

 f)

Question 7

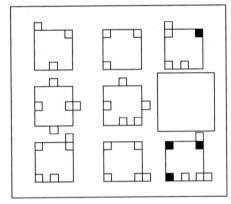

 a)

 b)

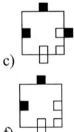 c)

 d)

 e)

f)

Question 8

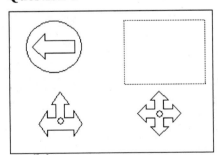

a)
b)
c)

d)
e)
f)

Question 9

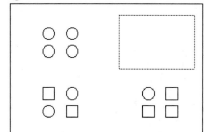

a)
b)
c)

d)
e)
f)

What are the missing numbers in the following patterns?

Question 10

33, ?, 29, 27, 25, ?...

a) 31, 23   b) 32, 24   c) 30, 24   d) None of these.

Question 11

-4, ?, -16, 32, -64, 128, ?...

a) -8, -256   b) 8, -256   c) 8, 256   d) None of these.

Question 12

2, 9, 23, ?, 107, ...

a) 47   b) 51   c) 53   d) None of these.

Question 13

89, ?, 87, 86, ?, 84, 83...

a) 88 and 81   b) 88 and 83   c) 87 and 85   d) None of these.

Question 14

7, 11, 19, 35, 67, ?, 259...

a) 134   b) 117   c) 131   d) None of these.

Question 15

A man punches into work at 1:45 pm and punches out at 3:30 am. How long was his shift?

a) 1:45   b) 10:30   c) 13:30   d) None of these.

Question 16

6 ½ minus 3 ¾ plus 4 ½ equals

a) 7 ½   b) 7 ¼   c) 7 ¾   d) None of these.

Question 17

A crate full of wheat weighs 60 kg. If 4 1/3 kg of wheat is spilled out of the crate, how much does the remaining wheat weigh?

a) 55 1/3   b) 55 2/3   c) 56 2/3   d) None of these.

Question 18

What number if doubled, gives you one quarter of 32?

a) 4   b) 8   c) 12   d) None of these.

Replace the asterisk with the missing number in the following questions.

Question 19

1	2	8
3	6	*
9		72

a) 16   b) 24   c) 32   d) None of these.

Question 20

12	15	
*	45	162
108		486

a) 48   b) 40   c) 36   d) None of these.

Question 21

49	77	
43	71	164
*	65	158

a) 40   b) 38   c) 34   d) None of these.

Question 22

275	55	*
50	10	2
	15	3

a) 5   b) 11   c) 15   d) None of these.

Question 23

	3	18
2	6	*
4	12	72

a) 32   b) 36   c) 42   d) None of these.

Question 24

If people spend two-thirds of their life awake, how many years would one spend sleeping if one lived to be 85 years old?

a) 24   b) 26   c) 28   d) None of these.

Question 25

In an electronic sale, a television was reduced by one-third from the original price. What was the original price if the new sales price is $70?

a) $ 116   b) $ 105   c) $ 100   d) None of these.

Question 26

A travel agent is allowed to reserve 5 rooms at any one booking. How many bookings are required to reserve 16 rooms?

a) 3   b) 5   c) 7   d) None of these.

Question 27

In a pizza eating contest a man can eat an eighth of his own weight in 45 minutes. If the man weighs 80 kg, how much can he eat in 30 minutes?

a) 5 1/3 kg   b) 5 2/3 kg   c) 6 1/3 kg   d) 6 2/3 kg

Question 28

Solve for "y" $21 + 15 \times 5 - y + 14 = 88$

a) 22   b) 25   c) 18   d) None of these.

Question 29

Solve for "y" $y - 42 = 103$

a) 61   b) 127   c) 144   d) None of these.

Question 30

Solve for "y" $20 + y \times 2 - 28 + 14 = 30$

a) 8   b) 12   c) 14   d) None of these.

Answer Key

Verbal

1) B
2) A
3) B
4) D
5) D
6) A
7) C
8) B
9) A
10) B
11) D
12) B
13) F
14) C
15) E

Spatial

1) B
2) A
3) A
4) D
5) A
6) A
7) C
8) B
9) A
10) C
11) D
12) B
13) A
14) A
15) B

16) C
17) B
18) B
19) B
20) A
21) B
22) A
23) D
24) B
25) C
26) B
27) D
28) D
29) C
30) B

31) A
32) A
33) C
34) A
35) C

Problem Solving

1) C
2) A
3) C
4) C
5) D
6) C
7) A
8) E
9) C
10) A
11) B
12) B
13) D
14) C
15) D

16) B
17) B
18) A
19) B
20) C
21) D
22) B
23) B
24) C
25) B
26) D
27) D
28) A
29) D
30) B

Verbal and Spatial tests – review the answer sheet.

Problem Solving Test

Question 1

521 x 346 = 180,266

Question 2

First subtract 4 hours from 1 pm, which brings you to 9 am. Then simply switch am to pm to subtract the remaining 12 hours. The answer is 9 pm.

Question 3

All of the products will cost a total of $42.24.

6 x $3.54 = $21.24   21.24 + 9.75 + 11.25 = 42.24

5 x $1.95 = $9.75

3 x $3.75 = $11.25

Then subtract the amount of the purchase from the dollars spent.

$50 – 42.24 = $7.76

Question 4

$\frac{15}{16}$ $\frac{7}{8}$ $\frac{3}{4}$ $\frac{2}{3}$ $\frac{1}{2}$ These fractions are all decreasing order. A sure way to check is to create a common denominator (48)

$\frac{45}{48}$ $\frac{42}{48}$ $\frac{36}{48}$ $\frac{32}{48}$ $\frac{24}{48}$

Question 5

The number of sides an object has keeps increasing by one.

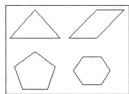

Question 6

Objects alternate between a circle and a circle with a cross (no colouring) on opposing corners.

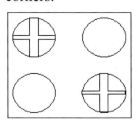

Question 7

Images from the first row are superimposed onto the second row, which results in the third row. Any overlap of small squares results in a colour change to black.

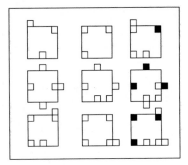

Question 8

The number of arrows is increasing by one each figure. The circles are internal on the bottom row and external on the top row.

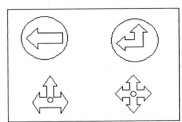

Question 9

The number of circles is decreasing by one and the number of squares is increasing by one.

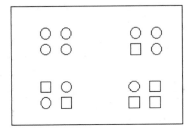

Question 10

The numbers are decreasing by 2 each time (33, 31, 29, 27, 25, 23...).

Question 11

The numbers are being multiplied by -2 (-4, 8, -16, 32, -64, 128, -256...).

Question 12

The numbers are being multiplied by 2 and added by 5 (2, 9, 23, 51, 107, ...).

Question 13

The numbers are decreasing by a factor of 1. (89, 88, 87, 86, 85, 84, 83...)

Question 14

The numbers are being multiplied by 2 and then subtracted by 3. (7, 11, 19, 35, 67, 131, 259...)

Question 15

The time between 1:45 pm and 3:30 pm is 1 and ¾ hours or 1:45 (3 2/4 – 1 ¾ = 1 ¾). You have to add another 12 hours for a total of 13 hours and 45 minutes (12:00 + 1:45 = 13:45).

Question 16

6 ½ = 6 2/4 = 26/4   3 ¾ = 15/4   4 ½ = 4 2/4 = 18/4

26 / 4 - 15 / 4 + 18 / 4 = 29 /4   =   7 ¼

Question 17

60 – 4 1/3 = 55 2/3 kg remain

Question 18

First determine what one-quarter of 32 is by dividing 32 by 4. 32 / 4 = 8. Next determine what number if doubled will give you 8. This is accomplished by dividing 8 by 2. The answer is 4 (8/2 = 4).

Question 19

Multiplying   2   4

3 ↓

1	2	8
3	6	24
9	18	72

Question 20

Multiplying

3 ↓

12	15	27
36	45	162
108	135	486

Question 21

Adding

6 ↑

49	77	170
43	71	164
37	65	158

Question 22

Multiplying   ←   5

275	55	11
50	10	2
75	15	3

Question 23

Multiplying   3   6

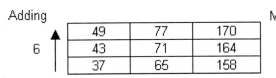

2 ↓

1	3	18
2	6	36
4	12	72

Question 24

If a person spends two-thirds of their life awake, then they must spend 1/3 of their life asleep. All you have to do is divide 85 by 3. One would sleep 28 years (85 / 3 = 28.3).

Question 25

An algebraic equation is required to answer this question. Let "y" equal the original price. Therefore if you subtract 1/3 (y) from the product, the answer would be 70.

$$y - 1/3 (y) = 70$$

$$2/3 (y) = 70$$

$$y = 70 \div 2/3 \quad \text{(multiply by the reciprocal)} \quad y = 70 \times 3/2 = 210 / 2 = 105$$

The original price was $105.

Question 26

Simply divide 16 by 5 (16 / 5 = 3.2). Because in 3 bookings you could at most book 15 rooms, you will require 4 bookings to reserve 16 rooms.

Question 27

First determine how many kilograms he can eat in 45 minutes. 1/8 of 80 kg is 10 kg (80 / 8 = 10).

Next calculate how much he can eat in 30 minutes. 30 is 2/3 of 45, so in order to solve the problem, you have to multiply 2/3 and 10 kg (10 x 2/3 = 20/3 = 6.66 or 6 2/3 kg).

Question 28

21 + 15 x 5 – y + 14 = 88

21 + 75 – y + 14 = 88

96 – y + 14 – 14 = 88 – 14

96 – 96 – y = 74 – 96

- y = - 22

y = 22

Question 29

y – 42 = 103

y – 42 + 42 = 103 + 42

y = 145

Question 30

20 + y x 2 – 28 + 14 = 30

20 + y x 2 – 14 = 30

20 + y x 2 – 14 + 14 = 30 + 14

20 – 20 + y x 2 = 44 – 20

y x 2 = 24

y x 2 / 2 = 24 / 2

y = 12